Wanted dead *and* alive!
Does that sound impossible? It is . . .
unless you're a Christian!
You still have a question?
Then this book is for you.
First you'll find out what it means to be dead—
dead to sin . . . buried with Christ.
Then you'll find out what it means to be alive—
alive in Christ . . . living abundantly.
Now living isn't easy, the book tells you that, too.
But living is possible. Want to know the secret?
Turn the pages, read, discover and then
Live, Christian, Live!

Live,
Christian, Live!

by Donald H. Gill

A Division of G/L Publications
Glendale, California, U.S.A.

ISBN 0-8307-0080-3

Second Printing, 1971

© Copyright 1970 by G/L Publications
Printed in U.S.A.

Published by
Regal Books Division, G/L Publications
Glendale, California, 91209, U.S.A.
All rights reserved

Library of Congress Catalog Card No. 71-117524
ISBN 0-8307-0080-3

Contents

A teaching and discussion guide for use with this book is available from your church supplier.

Contents

CHAPTER 1

HOW DO I GET STARTED?

Very few people are completely satisfied with their own way of life. For most people things move along from day to day in a routine pattern. Although there may be some high points as well as low, most of life for most people is a humdrum existence.

But that is not the way it was meant to be. Life was intended to be full and meaningful. Not necessarily easy. In fact, many of the people who have lived the most meaningful and satisfying lives, and who have contributed most to the world round them, have been people burdened with problems and pain. Just think of Abraham Lincoln, for instance.

How can life be full and meaningful—overflowing, as they say? The Bible says it can be.

Rendezvous

It is nighttime in a secluded spot in Jerusalem. Two men are engaged in an intense discussion. Although it started on a more-or-less philosophical level, it quickly moves into a discussion involving their own lives.

Then comes Jesus' bold declaration to Nicodemus, a leader of the Jewish people: You must be born all over again.

What nonsense is this? How can a man be born again when he is already a grown adult? Is this a jest? Is He putting me on?

Nicodemus must have quickly gathered that Jesus was quite serious. The explanation continued. This new birth is a thing of the Spirit. Physical birth is one thing. Spiritual birth is another. That which is born of the flesh is flesh, and that which is born of the Spirit is spirit.

Is the concept of a new birth—a spiritual birth—valid today?

The person whose life has been turned around spiritually is the best one to answer that question. Outside of the Scripture, and the words of Jesus, the best evidence comes from those who have experienced it. These are people who know what they are talking about.

They can be found from skid row to the highest offices in the land. They have a "specially alive" sense about them. They are in touch with God, and they are prepared for anything. They face life with an ultra-aliveness.

How does this come about? Is it the result of religious exercises they perform? Not usually. Is it some psychological approach to life which has helped them? Not really.

Then what has happened?

Although there are many ways of rationalizing it (those who have not experienced it have all sorts of explanations for it), the only real explanation is that God entered the scene, in a personal way. The faith that makes this happen is the faith that is placed in Jesus Christ, as God's sacrifice for man's sin.

The nighttime conversation between Jesus and Nicodemus involved the secret of the ages—the answer to all those who pursue life to the fullest. And it is all wrapped up in one Person. He was there that night giving Nicodemus an advance notice of the significance of His presence among men.

Who Qualifies?

We often have a miserable way of counting some people out. It may be their race that is our problem. Or, perhaps their religion. Or, their economic status. Or, most anything that makes them seem different from us.

In the case of Zacchaeus, it was his profession that caused the problem. He was a chief tax-gatherer, employed by the Romans. Since the Jews had moral and political reservations against the flow of tax money to Rome, they despised tax collectors.

And Zacchaeus, as a chief collector, was especially detested because he was a Jew who was deeply involved with the Roman tax system.

What's more, it is clearly indicated (see Luke 19:8) that injustice was involved in the collection system which Zacchaeus managed. All these things together put Zacchaeus at the top of the register of detestable people in Jericho. Although he was rich, he was an outcast.

It is interesting how Jesus gravitated to just that sort of person. When Zacchaeus' curiosity brought him out with the crowd, Jesus was quick to spot him—and of all things, asked Himself to dinner at Zacchaeus' house. How quickly Zacchaeus responded to this unexpected openness and acceptance on Jesus' part.

Jesus is the kind who goes against the grain of the social structure. Not to be offensive. He never sought to offend just for the sake of being negative. Rather He seemed impelled to make the incident a lesson in the way God looks at things.

God could not have been pleased with Zacchaeus' past record any more than the Jews were. But Jesus saw Zacchaeus' *potential*.

And that is where God meets you. And it is where we as Christians must meet others.

Why Do I Qualify?

Some things cannot be measured. Love is one of those things. It can be demonstrated, tested, communicated and felt. But there is no way to measure it.

Especially the love of God. So great is His love that everyone who gets a look at it is held in wonder and amazement. The highest demonstration of His love, of course, came in the sacrifice of Himself for the sin of men. At the crucifixion of Jesus Christ the whole world was allowed a glimpse of the Almighty in agony, sacrificially pouring out everything that was dearest to Him in order to make it possible that men could be restored to favor and fellowship with God.

While it is possible to state this, it is impossible to grasp it fully. Paul was wrestling with this fact in his letter to the church at Ephesus (3:14–21). He stated his hope that the Christians would somehow be able to comprehend the love of Christ.

Paul was undoubtedly concerned that they comprehend the love of God intellectually. But the passage indicates his concern that they also might know it in their daily experience.

Paul also mentioned the fact that a great family, the church in its universal sense, is bound together in the name of Jesus Christ. This is one thing it means to be Christian. We bear the name of Christ. And we are related to all those who likewise follow Him in faith and bear His name.

This is one aspect of the new life. It is not lived in isolation. Rather the Christian, like John Bunyan's allegorical Pilgrim, travels among many others who are likewise on a pilgrimage. They differ in their personalities and in the problems they confront, but all those who bear the name of Christ have a family connection and an ultimate goal in common.

Because God is the center of it, the new life is in some sense beyond comprehension. It is not something you can talk yourself into, although reason does have its place in approaching it. Yet it is something that is really only possible as the human soul reaches out in faith to accept what God has done in Jesus Christ.

Once faith really latches onto the fact that the individual can be directly related to God, as a son is related to his father, a whole new world opens up. The Christian begins his journey in this new world through faith, and he must continue in faith if his life is to continue to be full and fruitful.

God is able to do things far beyond our small scale of comprehension, as His power is able to go to work in us. And that is exactly what God wants to do if we will let Him.

I'm All Right as I Am!

There is something about human nature that seeks self-justification through good works. In everyone there is to be found that certain something that eventually works its way around to some attempt to justify itself.

Whenever a man stands to be judged he rationalizes his actions and points out to the judge the places where he has obeyed the law. Although he knows he is guilty, he attempts to justify himself. This is a sort of universal urge in all men. It is a reflex that is rooted in the sinner's knowledge that he is guilty.

Yet as Galatians 2:16 points out, nobody is ever

justified by keeping the law. The only route to justification is a very different one, and is founded on faith in the Person of Jesus Christ. In Him alone can men find justification with God. Many find this hard to believe, and in many cases this is because the person involved is still hanging on to some inner hope that he will be able to justify himself.

In a sense it is our ego that gets in the way. "I'll do it myself, Father" is the response of many millions of people to the suggestion that they should turn to God for salvation. Yet God says they cannot have it on those terms. The instinct that aims at self-sufficiency in all things must lie down and die at this point.

Thus Paul says "I am crucified with Christ." Yet that is not all there is to it, Paul adds, for I do go on living, but the life I now live is the life that Christ lives in me. Any living that I do is based on the faith that I have in Jesus Christ, the Son of God, who loved me and gave up His life so that I could live.

How many Christians really live that way? All too often Christian living adds up to little more than a series of Sunday activities. If a few other weekday activities can be included, fine. But that is certainly not what Paul was talking about. Rather he had a view that somehow Jesus took over his whole life. Jesus, living in him, related to everything, every act, every word, every motivation, every thought.

This did not mean that Paul was suddenly living at some superhuman level of existence. Indeed, he was well aware of his failings, his thorn in the flesh, his human weakness. But he had made a genuine transaction, and it evidently was taken seriously by both Paul and by the Lord. For Paul gave over his life, so that his whole system of motivation and action could be available to God.

And that is what God is looking for in His followers today. Total willingness to have God live in us. That is what He really wants. In fact, nothing else will do. If we hold back, even a part of ourselves, God is unable to carry through and work out His plans as He wants to—because we get in the way.

Seeing Me as I Am

Childhood is our introduction to life. Many of our ideas about the world and about life are derived from childhood experiences. Our ideas of a father, for instance. Or our views about work, recreation, worship, leadership and so on.

Discipline, or law, is another area in which we get early ideas about how things work, and how they ought to work. As children proper behavior was expected of us. If we got out of line, we were punished.

Then as we grew older we were expected to internalize that discipline, so that we could handle ourselves according to the rules of society around us. And when we have children of our own, we start the cycle of discipline all over again, by demanding that they adhere to the rules we make.

This process is natural and proper. But it involves a serious problem. The average person is apt to conclude that righteousness is nothing more or less than keeping rules. The good person is the person who keeps all the rules, according to this view.

Not so. Rules may keep a man from acting out the evil that he may want to perform. But they fail to inspire him to do good. At the level of motivation he still lives unto himself, and that is where the trouble begins.

And that is also where the new life enters. Jesus came to announce, and to make possible, a better way. This is a way that reaches down through the layers of man's callous self-centeredness and turns him around. He really becomes a new man when he accepts Jesus Christ.

On one occasion, Jesus was teaching about the law. He summarized it in just two points: Love God and love your neighbor. (See Matthew 22:37–40.)

Who follows that rule? Anyone you know? Not a chance. No man has ever loved God as fully as he should. And as for love to neighbors, who has ever kept that one fully?

Then we must ask: Was Jesus teaching nonsense in summarizing the law into two points that no man can keep fully? Not at all. For by this means man gets an idea of what he was meant to be—and what he is not. Thus he sees the disparity between the ideal and the reality, and this allows him to see his need.

And it is precisely that need which Jesus Christ came to solve.

Just seeing one's own need is a good beginning—

in fact, good enough that Jesus told the scribe: "Thou art not far from the kingdom of God."

Can I Please God?

"Love God and do as you please." That startling advice came from Augustine, one of the most influential leaders of the Christian movement, who lived in the fourth and fifth centuries.

At first the mind boggles at his advice. All of us know that human nature is always bent on doing what it pleases. And therein lies the problem of all men. The Bible tags it as sin. Doing what you please. And then becoming a prisoner of the things you do. Which becomes what pleases you. And so it develops into a maddening circuit of chasing what pleases you, but finding that when you have attained it, you are not so pleased after all.

But Augustine had that experience too. In his earlier years he had lived a dissolute, unregenerate life. Later he poured out his regrets and repentance in his *Confessions*. But then he said: "Love God and do as you please."

How could he? Is he out of line with Scripture? How would he defend his position? And how does this fit with Paul's advice in Ephesians?

The statement of Augustine is something like an optical illusion. The mind sees the wrong things at first, and therefore is disoriented to the whole meaning of the statement. It is always easiest for the mind to grasp something that involves human activity—the "do as you please" part. For some reason it is more difficult to grasp the simple directive: "Love God."

But that is the important part. That is where it all starts and where it finishes too, if you really understand it. Loving God is not a small matter. It is not a set of daily devotions, although that may help. It is not church attendance, or many other things that might be done to please God.

Love and faith are intimately related. "For he that cometh to God must believe that he is, and that he is a rewarder of them that diligently seek him" (Hebrews 11:6). That is something to go on. Seek a relationship to God and you have His word that you will get it, providing you really mean business.

Paul adds to this. He says: "Be ye therefore followers of God, as dear children" (Ephesians 5:1). Then he adds that we should live in love, just as Christ has loved us. Love God. Then the other things on the list that Paul cites will come naturally. In a sense, if you can follow what Augustine said, if you really love God completely, all of your life will shape up to please Him.

Do you love God that way? Nobody can boast that he has arrived. Even Paul admitted that. But when we think about it, our attitude toward God is really the place to begin.

Reborn Free

Most of us live in what we consider freedom.

To start with, we live in a free-world setting. The laws of our land allow us a great deal of free choice as regards our own activities. We can choose our work, our sports, our residence, our education, our political leadership, our friends, our way of worship, our dress and so on. This is freedom.

Or is it?

If that is our definition of freedom, many people around us may be free in theory but they are really living like slaves. Human desires and passions have a way of taking over. What started out to be a free choice turns out to be something that is dictated to us by the forces within. And we are helpless in changing those forces.

So we are free, but we are really prisoners—to ourselves and to the forces within ourselves.

What is the way out? Who can lead us to freedom?

Paul's letter to the Romans centers in the answer to this question. He points out that a new law is at work in the world. See Romans 8:1-9.

It is just as if we discovered some law that would counter the law of gravity. Imagine the results. People could do all sorts of new tricks.

Paul calls the new law "the law of the Spirit of life in Christ Jesus." And it operates in direct opposition to the law of sin and death. To be in the power of one is to be out of the grips of the other. This is real freedom: To choose to put ourselves in a field of force that can overcome all the other forces with which we have to contend, both outside and within us. And that is exactly what Paul is talking about.

This is the only way to live. It is the only kind of life that is really alive.

It is like flying. It is against the law of gravity. Wilbur and Orville Wright discovered that the laws of aerodynamics could overcome the usual results of the law of gravity—whatever it is about gravity that says that things heavier than air should stay on the ground. It took real faith and considerable daring on the part of the Wright brothers to attempt to fly, especially when so many others had attempted to imitate the birds and had failed.

Paul suggests exactly the same thing in the world of the Spirit. Every follower of Jesus Christ should learn to fly.

Live!

A new life is available to anyone who is seriously interested. It is a higher, more meaningful way of life than most people live today. Many people are so trapped by their past that they cannot imagine a new life is available. But it is! It is available from Jesus Christ who died to make it possible.

Today would be a good time for you to get started living. Right now stop reading and ask the Lord to give you this new life you have been discovering is possible. It is yours when you receive Jesus Christ as your Saviour.

With the Lord's gift of new life you are now a Christian. The rest of this book is for you. So read on. And "Live, Christian, Live!"

CHAPTER 2

WHO IS GOD TO ME?

Who is God? Where is He? Plenty of people these days would like to know.

In a way, the Greeks were in a similar search. At least they suspected that there may be some unknown deity of which they had not heard. When Paul spoke on Mars' Hill he was quick to affirm that this was indeed the case. But, he said, God could be known. He had revealed Himself in the person of His Son, whom He had raised from the dead.

Any hope of knowing God today must start at this same point, in the person of Jesus Christ, the central character of the whole biblical narrative.

Knowing God in a personal way can be life's

greatest adventure. It is the only way to a life that is really full and meaningful.

God, the Source

Christopher Columbus, Admiral Byrd and Neil Armstrong are names that will go on and on in history. These men discovered new worlds. They led the way to new areas of human experience. But these are not the only kinds of explorers. There are inner worlds of the spirit, and worlds of interpersonal fellowship, where every individual is an explorer in search of reality.

How many worlds are you in touch with? One index of the healthy personality is the ability to be in touch with a variety of fields of thought and experience. In this sense the Athenians who heard Paul on Mars' Hill were healthy people. They spent much time exploring new ideas.

But the problem was that they failed to arrive at the truth. Curiosity is a healthy trait when it is harnessed to a genuine search for truth. But idle curiosity is something else again. Just sifting through new ideas and irrelevant facts is no virtue in itself, especially if the exercise leads nowhere. This tended to be the problem of the Greek philosophic set.

Another problem is the tendency to get locked to ideas that are based on invalid assumptions. The Greeks had built up a whole mythological world of personal deities. But these pagan gods were finite and fallible.

Think of your friends. How many of them have locked onto ideas and values which turn out to be temporary or invalid? And what about your own value system? What is uppermost in your life? What is most important to you? This is always a good place to begin. It is the key to finding out who you really are.

The life that is out of touch with God is out of alignment with everything else. This is why Paul used the altar to the Unknown God as a basis for introducing the Athenians to the Creator of heaven and earth, in whom all life is rightly centered.

Thus there is both a plus and minus potential in curiosity—the exploratory instinct—depending where it is headed. To the person who is rooted in God's love in Jesus Christ, life itself can become a daily adventure with God.

How do you feel about life? Is it a bore? If so, perhaps you should consider the alternative. If God, as a part of your day-to-day experience, has been something of an unknown quantity to you, why not open up to Him? What have you to lose?

God, the Strength

A curious thing happens whenever a person discovers God. He finds out that long ago God discovered him. The fresh experience of God's love is the clue that he was "chosen in him before the foundation of the world" (Ephesians 1:4).

Can this really mean what it says? God surely could not love me before I existed. This is the human reaction to the statement. But the human mind cannot possibly comprehend the mind of God. If we say we cannot understand how He does it, we are exactly right. Nobody can fully understand it. But anyone can respond to it, and that is what is important. God chose us to be His own.

What God wants is recognition—the kind of recognition that accepts His love and attempts to return it, at least in some measure. His love is perfect, ours is always imperfect. But God wants our love just the same.

How can we recognize a Spirit-being? We have only our senses to go by. How can we understand God when we have such limited means of perception?

God chose to become visible to humans. His visibility was in the person of Jesus Christ. This is the primary means by which we know God. We meet Him personally in Jesus. This is the essential and central point of the Bible. God revealed Himself in Christ, and in His death and resurrection we have the basis of a renewed relationship with God—the relationship that was broken by sin.

What God really wants is a relationship—one in which He is counted in, as the party of the first part. The whole contract begins with Him. Yet, in practice, He is usually left out of the whole thing. This is where repentance comes in. Broken relationships cannot be mended without genuine apologies and the desire for forgiveness.

Have you ever experienced that deep inner desire to be related to life, to the very essence of it? Probably everyone does at some time or other. It could be the voice of the Spirit, asking you to seek Him out. But it can be much more than a passing feeling. It can be a constant in your experience—the knowledge of being a child of God, and therefore related to all that He is doing in the world. Is that what you want?

God, the Wisdom

Children can teach us a lot. It is too bad we do not learn more easily from them. Children are always discovering, opening up to new relationships. They explore the relationship to parents and to brothers and sisters. Then come friends, teachers and so on.

Christians are much the same. They too are discovering. They explore relations with God, with other Christians, with those who have studied and experienced God's goodness—not only in good times but in bad as well.

It is a tragic fact that all too many Christians settle down to a substandard way of life sometime after their initial experience of God's love. The Lord later warned the church at Ephesus: "Nevertheless I have somewhat against thee, because thou has left thy first love" (Revelation 2:4).

How sad! Here is the picture of the couple who have been enthralled with each other, so much so that they have experienced a whole new dimension of life in being together. But after a while they let their relationship deteriorate. It withers. They are not alive to each other as they once were.

The best time to repair anything is before the damage is too great. After things deteriorate over a long period of time, the problem always increases. Each passing day counts.

Listening is a very important part of any relationship. It is enlightening. You really discover the other person when you listen. There is great fellowship in listening, especially on a one-to-one basis.

Listening to God need not be something overly mystical. Angelic messengers, ghostly presences, writing on the sky and special signs are not God's usual way of speaking. In fact, anything of that sort needs to be watched with great care because it can be misleading. Always be sure to "try the spirits whether they are of God" (I John 4:1).

The spirits can be tested by God's Word. If their message is out of line with Scripture, watch out. How much better to pray for the "spirit of wisdom and revelation in the knowledge of him" (Ephesians 1:17). This is the ground for real enlightenment.

God, the Energy

Aliveness! That is what everyone wants. Who would not be eager to be vitally alive? Who is willing to simply exist? In the language of the campus, "Here's where it's at!"

People today, especially young people, are resorting to all sorts of measures to become more alive. Drugs, alcohol, risk rides, trips, sex and so on. All these, and a good many more, are being tried as means of "turning on."

Is there any sure route to aliveness? Does Christ want to "turn people on"? To that question the Bible gives a clear answer. Yes.

God "quickened" these Christians to whom Paul was writing. (See Ephesians 2:1.) He made them alive. What could be more clear, or more relevant to the search for aliveness going on around us today?

These people had been dead. They were the captives of their own past.

Life, at the level it is usually lived, has a way of getting to us. It drags us down. Our own personal passions become everything. There is no room left for anything else. We become prisoners of ourselves, our desires, our vanities, our pleasures, and even our ideas of what is worthwhile.

Emancipation is the only answer. We need to be set free—free from ourselves. Life can never be lived fully when it is self-centered. It is more apt to be a living death. Yet this is the experience of millions and millions of people in our world today. Many are ready and willing to admit it.

It is a shame that so many people have missed this basic element in the Christian message. This is partly the fault of the church. It has often failed to demonstrate aliveness itself. The life and practice of the church have so often just become a set of formal activities. Vitality is missing.

God, the Renewer

Thought patterns have a way of becoming habitual. Usually they are dictated by a system of personal motivation rooted in the subconscious. Conscious choice often gives way to habitual response.

As Paul points out to the Ephesian Christians, the ordinary course of habitual living is at a terribly low level. (See 4:18–20.) And in this respect, times have not changed. The same way of life Paul described is evident all around us.

Where do people find their way of living? What produces a culture? How are values shared? These are complicated questions. Books have been written in answer to them.

One thing can be said in brief. Man instinctively lives at the low level of human nature—fallen human nature. He is not naturally in possession of godly instincts. These must be brought to him from the outside, through a relationship with God.

In other words, a man needs a new mind, a new outlook, a new orientation to life. This is what Paul says these Christians have experienced through their relationship to Jesus Christ. They have experienced a mental renewal. "Be renewed in the spirit of your mind," he says.

This should not be taken to mean that Christians never face problems. Not so! Christians probably have as many problems to face as anyone else. But they have more resources with which to face them. Here again is where the new mind comes in.

The new mind—the new mental set, if you like—is rooted in a relationship to God. He is the one really in control. He is in control of the entire universe and of the individual life which is submissive to His will. This is the person who lives more fully. Through God, he is related to all of life.

God, the Director

Circumspection is the ability to look around to see where you are, to choose the next step properly, and to please God in doing so. When you stop to think about it, that is quite an accomplishment.

But it is not a one time thing. You need to keep it up, and that makes it much more of an accomplishment! In fact, it is impossible. Nobody can expect to keep up a record of choosing the right step every time, unless. . . .

Who has the key to wisdom? Who knows where things are headed? What source of understanding can really be trusted?

Again we come back to God. Paul talks about "understanding what the will of the Lord is" (Ephesians 5:17). Is this some mystical knowledge, off somewhere in the heavenlies, only to be brought down to earth through some system of spiritual maneuvers? Not really. There are times, of course, when God wants us to get aside with Him for some extended period in order to know His mind on some matter. This is not because God is in doubt about what to do or where to go. It is usually God's way of having us experience a deeper level of fellowship with Him, and to make us quite clear about what He is trying to do in our lives.

Most of the time the will of the Lord is more like a set of operational assumptions that guide us from day to day. From Scripture we get a pretty good idea when we please Him, and when we don't. For instance, it is clear from this section in Ephesians that we please God when we use time wisely, in activities which glorify God.

When you have a few minutes it might be helpful for you to sit down and list the various ways in which you know God has been building and using your life. Then you can get a feel for the "trend lines"—the direction in which He is developing you.

God, the Stabilizer

Is anything of enduring value? Those who inhale the mood of despair, which characterizes so much of life today, would say no. They have given up hope of finding anything that seems to them transcendent or beyond the nitty-gritty world of here and now.

To this Paul says: "We look not at things which are seen, but at the things which are not seen: for the things which are seen are temporal; but the things which are not seen are eternal" (II Corinthians 4:18).

This is a strange but illuminating statement. The unseen is what is really real. Everything that can be seen, as a part of this world system, is of passing significance only. Anyone who takes this seriously will have some radically different attitudes toward life around him. His values system will be inverted.

It was because of this inverted value system that Paul could maintain his attitude toward his afflictions. The ordinary man would long since have sunk into the depths of self-pity if he had to endure the pain and the problems mentioned by Paul. But they were only slight momentary afflictions to him. In fact, he was not particularly troubled that the outward man should perish, because the inner man was the real man.

How many people do you know who really look

at things this way? What is distinctive about their reactions to life? How did they come to their viewpoint?

Sometimes it is easier to see what people are made of when some particular problem strikes them. A death in the family, a hospitalization, the loss of a job or some other problem can strike any of us at any time. At times like these our values are really tested. Our idea of what is worthwhile becomes visible.

Ask yourself how you might react if some specific calamity were to strike you suddenly. What would be your natural reaction? Would it be in line with Paul's idea of what was really real? What could you do to make yourself more aware of the "far more exceeding and eternal weight of glory" to which Paul had set himself?

All around us people are searching for reality, for aliveness, for relatedness. God has answers for anyone who will listen.

Yet it is also true that God has chosen direct personal means through which to convey the answers. The Word of God must become real in individual lives. And when it does, it seeds itself down in the lives of others.

Are you willing to be on the receiving end of the life that is vitally alive in Jesus Christ? And then will you be a channel through which God can communicate that life to others?

CHAPTER 3

AM I WORTH ALL THIS?

The rush and hustle of the Christmas season often keep us from fully appreciating the meaning of Christ's birth. What is even more unfortunate is the fact that these same activities keep us from sharing with others the wonderful truth of what God has done for us in Christ.

The Scriptures ring with praises to God whenever the birth of Christ is mentioned. Down through the corridors of the centuries you can hear the voices of great throngs of Christians singing with the angels: "Glory to God in the highest."

The Gift of Light

Darkness is abhorrent. It is abominable.

Children fear it, and cry for the light. Only after adjustment and accommodation do they accept the dark. Yet there may come a time when the grown man prefers the darkness, because it tends to hide his evil deeds.

It covers up his real self. The only way he can live with himself is by not facing what he really is. Therefore, the darkness becomes his friend. The tables have turned and the light is his enemy. Now the light is abhorrent.

But man's only hope is the light. He is destined to vanity, frustration and eventually to damnation as he resides in the darkness, never daring to face the truth.

It is within this world of darkened men that there comes an announcement.

Light!

Light has made its breakthrough into the world. The early glimmer, far over the horizon, had been witnessed by the prophets of the Old Testament. But the sunrise really took place at Bethlehem. And only a few people—lovers of the light—were there to see it.

And the sunrise was good news. It meant life. The warmth of the sun was felt by crowds of people on the hillside in Galilee. Even in the streets of Jerusalem there were some who recognized, at least for a brief moment, the beauty of the sun.

But the lovers of darkness were repulsed. They sought to smother the Light, to discredit it, to banish it as an influence in the world. And on Calvary it seemed they had succeeded, for the Light gave way to darkness.

But then came another sunrise—the most glorious sunrise of all. Another announcement, He is risen. And over the countryside poured the most beautiful dazzling Light that man had ever witnessed. A few more were there to see it this time, and they rejoiced together.

They became worshipers of the Light. They spread the word about its coming. What matter the threats of the lovers of darkness? We have the Light, they said. And they had lives that proved it. They radiated the Light to everyone in reach.

And others looked and found it to be true. Light was come.

"That was the true Light, which lighteth every man that cometh into the world" (John 1:9).

The Gift of His Favor

Who doesn't know the feeling of being favored—being the favorite, even temporarily, of teacher, manager, lover, leader or potentate? What a thrill!

But what of being favored by God? That is His grace. It is available to anyone who seeks it, providing he looks in the right place. And the right place is a person.

Jesus Christ is the embodiment of God's grace. Apart from Jesus there was no basis for grace, no possibility of reconciliation. But in Him came the fullness of grace.

Prior to that time, in the period of the Old Testament, men had seen glimpses of God's grace. But it was only a glimpse now and then. Until the coming of Jesus Christ, God appeared more austere and demanding. Most men had not come to know God very well.

But it was not His purpose to hide His real nature for ever. On the contrary, He was waiting for the right moment in which to reveal Himself to men. And this was the moment. "But when the fullness of the time was come, God sent forth his Son, made of a woman" (Galatians 4:4).

In some events, timing is everything. There is a proper time for the cake to come from the oven, a proper time for the egg to hatch, a proper time for the young bird to be pushed from its nest, and a proper time for the child to be born. God is a setter of times.

For His own coming into the world there was a time—and now the fullness of time had come.

Grace was put on display.

And truth.

For Jesus Christ also embodied the truth of God. He said, "I am the way, the truth, and the life" (John 14:6).

It is in Jesus that men get a true look at God, and at His grace. Not in the Law. Not in prophetic utterances. Not in the passing appearance of God's presence. But rather in the person of Jesus Christ.

This was what men could understand, what they could identify with, what they could see, listen to and follow. This was the Person.

"Grace and truth came by Jesus Christ" (John 1:17).

The Gift of Himself

Children are born every day. It happens all the time. So, what is so special about the birth of a single child? Nobody runs down to the hospital and peeks through the nursery window just to see any new baby who might have been born.

But when it's *your* child, that's something different. You will be there. It is a great milestone in your life. You will remember it, and you will delight in this moment of new life entering the world.

There are times when whole nations await the birth of a particular child—usually the child of the king, or of the president. These too can be moments of significance.

But there is no birth as significant as the birth of the Son of God.

And under such grim circumstances! Unbelievable!

Luke gives us the details. The mother, in labor, is turned away from the inn, gives birth to her child in a cave and wraps Him in swaddling clothes and lays Him in the manger. The Son of God, no less! Unbelievable! But true.

The wonder of that story will never wear out. There is something fresh and new and very beautiful about it every time we hear it.

God's Son was born in Bethlehem.

And the world looked the other way.

But the angel had already given instructions to Joseph. After explaining that the child had been conceived of the Holy Spirit, the angel stated flatly that it would be a Son, and that they should name the child Jesus—"for he shall save his people from their sins," the angel said.

Jesus.

God, our Saviour.

Nobody else in all the world can save people from their sins. And here He is, laid in a manger in Bethlehem.

What wonder!

What love!

What grace!

Unwelcomed

Getting attention is no small matter. Life is so filled with pressures, and so filled with ruts and routines that people just won't listen. They are too involved with the mundane details of their own existence.

No wonder they miss Jesus. The details of their existence leave no time for anything of importance, or even for the things that are all-important. Life has become so twisted that most people cannot sort out the really important things. The things that look so important are temporary, it turns out. And the things that are passed over are the things that are of highest significance.

Even God fails to get people's attention.

And that is not new.

He has had trouble that way before—through no fault of His own.

But then there are a few—and so often it's the commoners, the simple, uncomplicated people who are open to God—who hear the message.

In the case of the birth of the Lord Jesus it was the shepherds, tending their flocks in the fields. The night sky was suddenly lighted with an angelic presence, and these men were notified that they were to be witnesses to the birth of the Saviour.

The angel added the specifications of the event so that there would be no mistake. The child would be born in Bethlehem, the city of David.

The sign would be unmistakable. They would find the baby wrapped in swaddling clothes lying in a manger. Today we sing about it as "the birth-place of the King." That night it was just a cave in Bethlehem—yet the sign of the presence of Christ, the Saviour.

Further evidence of the significance of the event was the heavenly host, appearing with the angel, and singing the praises of God and good news to men.

Yet it was only a few shepherds who saw what was really happening. And it is only a few today who fully understand the significance of Jesus Christ among men. Like the residents of Bethlehem most people sleep through it all. But God goes on doing His wonders among men.

Unrecognized

Born in a rocky stable.

Destined to be leader of a great nation and the commander of forces that would move the world.

That is the basic portrait of Jesus Christ.

And those who waited for the Messiah, as predicted for hundreds of years, didn't even notice when

He came on the scene. They missed Him. For His kingdom was not of this world.

God's plan was larger than anything man could imagine. And it still is, but a few basic facts have filtered through to us, from Jesus Himself and from the Scriptures.

Some of the clues come from Isaiah 55.

"Ho, every one that thirsteth." God would provide the answer to man's thirst, Isaiah suggested. Then hundreds of years later, by a well in Samaria, Jesus said: "Whosoever drinketh of the water that I shall give him shall never thirst; but the water that I shall give him shall be in him a well of water springing up into everlasting life" (John 4:14).

Then Isaiah asked his people: "Wherefore do ye spend money for that which is not bread?" And hundreds of years later Jesus, speaking to His followers about the manna in the wilderness, broke through to the deeper meaning of things and declared to them: "I am the bread of life: he that cometh to me shall never hunger" (John 6:35).

Isaiah was speaking of things that were beyond him in any sense of complete understanding, but he spoke faithfully the words of God and in due time they fit into the whole picture as only God could arrange it.

Isaiah even predicted the opening up of the gospel in its availability to all men. "Behold, thou shalt call a nation that thou knowest not, and nations that knew not thee shall run unto thee . . . for the Holy One of Israel . . . hath glorified thee" (Isaiah 55:5). Here is the picture of people from all parts of the world turning to Jesus Christ.

Amid all this Isaiah declares that Christ would be a leader of a great nation—the nation of the redeemed—which would turn to God. He would be a commander of forces that would move the world for God.

And He was born in a stable!

Without Honor

The contrast is stark and beautiful. Look at the setting in Bethlehem. From the human standpoint, only a very few people recognized and honored the King. Most of the world passed Him by.

Yet He was appointed by God to receive "honor and glory," as Peter points out (II Peter 1:17).

He did receive honor and glory, even though it was witnessed only by the few. They were the ones privileged to see the King, even in the baby. The shepherds were there. And the wise men from the east came later, and were perhaps even then beginning their journey, carrying their gifts of gold, and frankincense and myrrh.

His parents were already party to the wonderful proportions of the event. And in the Temple, Simeon and Anna rendered their praise and thanksgiving to God.

But few others recognized Him.

There was, of course, the most significant recognition of all—the heavenly choir that rendered its praise to God for what He was doing in bringing His Son into the world.

Honor implies the complete righteousness and the magnanimous character of God.

Glory focuses attention on the brilliancy of God's achievement.

In sending His Son into the world God solved, once and for all, the problem of man's sin. He found the way, through Christ's death and resurrection, to cover man's sin and to preserve His own righteousness. Thus, to those who believe, and who thereby appropriate God's grace, salvation and reconciliation are assured.

This is the drama of the ages. This is the focal point of history. This is the resolution of the sin problem among men.

But only the few were there to give God honor and glory at His birth. And only the few recognized who He was during His life on earth. Only the few recognized what was taking place as He went to the cross, and only the few believed when He rose again from the dead.

It is only the few who really accept Him for what He is today. It is only the few who look forward to His return, and to His judgment of men and nations. But God is pleased with the few.

To Him belong honor and glory.

Triumphant

From the beginning of time most men have been subject to the changing whims of those who occupy the roles of leadership. The affairs of nations often hang on personal motivations such as pride, desire for territory or power, revenge, greed, and the craving for riches and acclaim.

Throughout history man has wished for peace.

But even while he wished for it he has been ensnared in war. Honor must be defended. Territory must be held. Land and possessions must be safeguarded. So a man chooses war rather than surrender to the greed of others who threaten him.

And peace goes begging.

The confused noise of battle rises again.

Garments rolled in blood are brought home from the field, with the memories of those who died.

Even when the war is finished, no permanent peace is guaranteed. Man enters into despondency and then despair. Who will bring peace? Who will raise a standard against war? Who can deliver from the threats that carry men into battle. Who will bring order to the affairs of men and nations?

In the distance Isaiah hears a shout from heaven. "Unto us a child is born, unto us a son is given: and the government shall be upon his shoulder: and his name shall be called Wonderful, Counsellor, The mighty God, The everlasting Father, The Prince of Peace" (Isaiah 9:6).

A new ruler is coming to power. The prince is waiting in the wings to ascend the throne. He will take over from the unlawful tyrant who has been in control. And He will provide for peace among men. He will bring order to the nations. His kingdom will constantly increase in power, and His rule will never end.

What a picture!

What a promise!

Isaiah was looking down through the ages, as God gave him to see, at least dimly, the outline of that era in which Jesus Christ would return as King.

In the telescoping effect of time there are many centuries in focus here. But the view of the kingdom is yet ahead, yet to be experienced by the world and by the church. But the time draws closer. This picture which Isaiah saw will become a reality.

The Prince of Peace is coming.

And peace and order shall be established.

Without Cost to Me

Light, life, grace, provision, peace—all gifts to us from God! But stop and consider the price the Lord Jesus paid to make them available. The God of glory came into our world, lived and died to make the gifts available. He rose again and showed that the price was paid and God would give His gifts to anyone who comes and asks for them.

In the light of all that Christ did, only one response seems possible—receive Him and His gifts. Then, consider "Am I worth all that it cost?" In the light of the answer, what do you think you should do?

CHAPTER 4

HOW AM I TO BE DIFFERENT?

Most Christians realize, at least in theory, that the Christian life is meant to be distinctive. It is not the same as the life of the world around it.

But *how* is it different?

That is the question that is harder to answer. And in response to it, all sorts of different opinions are offered. There is little consensus on what should be the nature of the ideal Christian life.

The best model to go by is still the original one. Jesus Christ. It is impossible to improve on Him as an example of the difference between the man of God and the world.

Throughout this chapter, it will be helpful to keep that in mind.

Me, Righteous?

"He was so good he would pour rose-water on a toad." That was what Douglas Jerrold the English playwright and humorist had to say about the "Charitable Man."

His witty comment is quite typical of popular reaction to righteousness.

So often, righteousness seems impractical, and rather out of this world. It is sometimes written off as "do-goodism." Somehow the connotation of righteousness has come unglued from the qualities of courage, strength and virility. Before you agree read I Peter 3:8–16.

One big reason why righteousness is not popular today is the fact that it has been under severe attack. A whole generation has arisen which has deliberately questioned the standards of righteousness which have been held by previous generations.

And with considerable reason.

The morality of war has been questioned, for instance. Even the most militaristic Christians admit it would be much better if there were no war. So it comes down to a question of how to handle international disputes and enforce justice and guarantee freedom without war. But even in wrestling with this question, we allow that the problem of war is a real one.

The standards of sex morality have been questioned widely in recent years—in fact, to the point where it appears that the whole structure of sex morality as we have known it in western cultures is about to crumble.

In place of the older standards some have proposed a "new morality." This is usually defined as a system that is based only on love—that is, on concern for the total effect of one's actions upon others.

This love is an unavoidable demand on the Christian, but the problem with this revised definition of love is the fact that it is extremely difficult to predict the "total" effect of one's actions. Another problem is that the motivation of love can itself become clouded, for it is so difficult for any man to know himself.

The Christian cannot set aside the demands of love—to that extent he identifies with the stated intent of the "new morality." But the Christian has something else to go by, something that helps fill in the meaning of love in real life.

Jesus Christ. He is our model of love.

And Loving, Too?

"Peace on earth to men of good will."

That is a phrase often repeated. But it is so often uttered with a minimal understanding of "men of good will."

Who are they? Anyone with good intentions? Good people? Good leaders? Those who try to pursue peace among the nations?

The biblical text reads "men in whom God is pleased!" And this just makes it more of a puzzle. For there is much Scripture to suggest that no man is pleasing to God. "All have sinned, and come short of the glory of God" (Romans 3:23).

So how can God be pleased with certain men, when all men are unpleasing to Him?

Perhaps the best way to solve the riddle is to see it in its total context. As Jesus Christ came into the world, the angels sang: "Glory to God in the highest, and on earth peace, good will toward men" (Luke 2:14). The entry of Jesus Christ into the world was to result in two things: Glory to God in the highest heavens, and on earth the introduction of peace, or reconciliation, to men whom God favors.

This was not deserved.

It was not earned.

It was the love of God poured out on undeserving men. If men had deserved God's love it still would have been great. But the real greatness of His love rests in the fact that it was totally undeserved.

In Luke 6 we find that Jesus follows up this thought and indicates that this sort of godly love is also to be characteristic of His followers.

Christians, like God the Father, are expected to offer the world love, even when it is not in any way deserved.

In fact, it is in circumstances where love is not deserved that it is really proved. And this is what Jesus is getting at. The distinctiveness of Christian love is demonstrated in the ability to love an enemy. This is impossible without understanding, and participating in, the kind of love that God has for men. "But God commendeth his love toward us, in that, while we were yet sinners, Christ died for us" (Romans 5:8). God "displayed" His love through Jesus Christ's death. He proved it once for all time.

The rest follows.

If we accept God's love, can we do any less than put it on display in our own lives?

Completely Honest?

Few people could lay claim to personal righteousness to the extent of the rich young man in Matthew 19:16.

When Jesus made a list of the commandments, this young man could reply, "All these things have I kept from my youth up." And it seems he was quite sincere in his response. Undoubtedly he had made a life-long attempt at exemplary righteousness.

Yet something was lacking.

Evidently he realized it, for he asked Jesus, "What lack I yet?"

Do you know how he felt?

Do you share the feeling of something still lacking? If so, you have much company. There are many signs that this is a common feeling in contemporary culture—the church included.

Notice Jesus' response when the young man asked what more he could do. Christ went right to the heart of the matter. He touched the one soft spot in this man's armor of righteousness.

He was wealthy.

He knew it, and he was happy in it. He delighted in his possessions, and in the power that they represented.

This was his point of weakness.

And he went away sorrowful.

We are not told in Scripture whether this young man ever came back to Jesus. Some think he did, and that he became one of the leaders of the early Christian church. Others conjecture that he went down into a miserable life of sin, delighting in his wealth—and captive to it.

We do not know.

But we do know that at this point in his experience, when he met Jesus, he was touched at the point where it really counted. And that was because Jesus knew him. God knew his heart.

Although he had kept most of the law in letter, he had missed it in spirit. Could he really love his neighbor as himself and refuse to share his wealth with those in great need? This one point showed his weak spot—his lack of integrity.

And when he saw himself, he was saddened.

God demands complete integrity.

It is impossible to please God by tallying up a list of things you have done right. God sees the heart. He knows what you are made of, and what you really think.

And that is where all of us are caught short.

The entry to integrity is through God's redemption in Jesus Christ.

And Sacrificial?

"Let my heart be broken by the things that break the heart of God." Those were the words written on the flyleaf of the Bible of Dr. Bob Pierce, founder of World Vision. They expressed his willingness to experience agony, if that were God's will. And Bob Pierce did experience agony on many occasions, but out of that agony came a continuing service to mankind in the name of Jesus Christ.

Agony and sacrifice are harsh words.

No man in his right mind invites agony or deprivation . . . unless . . .

Imagine the prospective disciple mentioned in Luke 9:57,58. He is almost swept off his feet by the great miracles, by the public response of the crowds, and by the thought that he might gain greatness through association with Jesus. And he promises to follow Jesus wherever He goes.

But Jesus knows his heart. He penetrates his inner motivation.

"Don't fool yourself," Jesus says, in effect. "The picture won't turn out to be what you think." Ahead was work, weariness, deprivation, loneliness, and eventually death. No glamor in that. It would be human nature to become accustomed to the crowds, and even weary of them. The disciples who were already following Jesus had wished more than once that the crowds would go away.

It became possible for them to see the crowds and not the people.

But not Jesus.

It is a matter of perspective.

He saw through human tendencies to get things out of perspective. So He put it directly to this young man: "You had better face the fact that I don't have as much of a home as the animals and birds of the field or forest." That must have made him think.

Jesus was not fooling anybody. As He asked another to follow Him the man asked to first arrange for his father's funeral. But Jesus warned: "let the dead bury the dead." If family or friends, or even respect for a departed loved one would keep you from being with Christ, then your relationship to Him is handicapped by the circumstances. And you cannot allow anything to come between you and Christ.

It is top priority or it is nothing at all.

Serving?

What title does the job carry?

That is about the first consideration of many men considering a new job. Even the salary may sometimes be considered only after the title is settled.

And the title must be symbolic of rank.

After all, if a man is going to pour his energies into a job, he deserves the distinction of a title that implies high status in the organization, and in society at large. That's how the reasoning goes, at least in many cases.

It even affected two of the disciples. See Matthew 20:20–23.

And their mother, no less.

Zebedee was probably quite wealthy. And there

is indication that his wife, Salome, the mother of James and John, may have supplied some of the financial support for Jesus, and perhaps some of the needs of the disciples. Taking this into account, and also the closeness of her sons to Jesus, it was reasonable in one sense for Salome to suggest that James and John should be top administrators in the kingdom that Jesus was to set up.

But Jesus had to tell this well-intentioned mother that she didn't know what she was asking. Salome didn't have the proper perspective. Her motivation was human, and very shortsighted.

Salome's request had stirred resentment among the other ten disciples, and Jesus called them together to discuss it. "Look," He said in essence, "most government systems work that way. You shouldn't be surprised by that sort of status-seeking. The only thing is, My kingdom won't run that way. In fact, anyone who wants top rank in My kingdom must become the least servant of all."

Jesus wasn't just saying this.

It was not a temporary expedient to relieve a tense situation. It was a fact built into the reality of God's way of working among men. It was the design for His kingdom, settled before the foundation of the world.

Service.

The servant attitude.

That is what counts. If anyone desires to do great things for the Lord, let him become the servant of every other Christian, not in name alone, but in daily activity.

Jesus practiced it Himself. "Even . . . the Son of

man came not to be ministered unto, but to minister [serve]" (Matthew 20:28). And this sort of living is costly.

Expendable?

Life grows out of death.

At the roots of the potato plant one can find the "old spud"—rotted away, perhaps hardly distinguishable amid the new potatoes. But out of it has sprouted the potato plant. And as it grew, it developed a new generation after its own kind.

The same principle runs throughout all plant life. The acorn dies, but brings forth an oak. The peach stone in the ground cracks open and disintegrates, but from it comes a new peach tree.

Likewise with corn and wheat and oats and rye and so on.

And Jesus uses this as an illustration of the Christian life.

"Except a corn of wheat fall into the ground and die, it abideth alone: but if it die, it bringeth forth much fruit" (John 12:24).

So far so good.

But when Jesus gets to the point of applying this principle to the Christian, the going becomes rough. It is clear that Jesus meant the Christian to identify with the "corn of wheat" that gives up its life.

He fulfilled that identity Himself, when He went to the cross.

All sorts of questions leap into our minds at that point. How can I give up my life? What am I worth without life? How can I serve God without life? Does God really want me to die?

Yes, He wants you to die.

There is no other way to understand the gospel. Christ first died for us. But then throughout the New Testament we find that Christians who were effective were those who identified with Jesus Christ in His death. They were reckless enough to throw their lives away—to act as if the life right here and now (this day-to-day existence that so often means everything in the world to us) meant nothing to them at all.

In fact, they were already dead.

Nobody could threaten them or harm them. Nobody could intimidate them. Nobody could influence them by the threat of hardship, or torture, or even death.

You simply cannot intimidate a dead man.

And they were dead men.

And the church grew out of their faithfulness in identifying with Jesus Christ in His death.

And nothing has changed, except the attitude of the followers.

If the church is to survive the present wave of secularism, if it is to be vital and meaningful in modern times, it will have to get back to the principle of death through which you find new life.

Christian, you sign your own death warrant. You are expendable!

In Training?

Here's another word that cuts against the grain.

Discipline.

Today we're not interested in discipline. Freedom, yes. But not discipline. That's out. At least not Christian discipline.

Perhaps discipline in sports.

That figures. If you hope to get into the Olympics, you are going to have to train. And if that's what you mean by discipline, all right, we'll agree to that.

But not in the Christian life. That sounds like a great big dose of religion, and that doesn't taste so good. Yet that is exactly the analogy that the writer of Hebrews uses in chapter 12:1,2. The race. It is the metaphorical window through which he sees the Christian life.

First there is the multitude in the grandstands. The heavenly witnesses. The great throng of those who have served God and who died without seeing the completion of the plan of God in Jesus Christ. These multitudes are the spectators, and they silently urge us on to the completion of the race.

Then there is the excess baggage that must be set aside. Nothing that will hamper can be allowed. Track shorts are the uniform. Nothing but the essentials.

Which of us can bring ourselves to leaving all the other things behind. For some reason we feel we can run the race with all sorts of other interests —the little sins that so easily wear us out.

Then there is the need to develop a steady pace. Run with patience. The runner that cannot pace himself cannot stand up under competition. Experience helps him know his own energies and only as he exerts those energies in a steady pace can he hope to win.

And the secret of running is in looking ahead to the goal—to the person of Jesus Christ. It is Christ who draws us on. As we get closer to Him we run harder, straining every spiritual muscle to gain the prize of pleasing Him. The end of the race is worth the extra sprint.

Run.

Run for the crowd that watches.

But, above all, run for Christ Jesus the King.

The quality of the Christian life, as it is lived from day to day, depends entirely on the ingredients you put into it.

Why not look back over the ingredients in this chapter and rate yourself on each item. Make a scale as follows:

Righteous

| 0 | 1 | 2 | 3 | 4 | 5 | 6 | 7 | 8 | 9 | 10 |

Then check (as above) where you rate yourself on each item, with 10 representing an "unbeatable" score, starting with "righteous," then "loving" and so on through the seven items.

Finally after seeing which item needs the most attention, see where you can begin to improve. Go back over the chapter if necessary. Then see where improvement can be achieved on the other items as well.

CHAPTER 5

WHAT IS THE BIBLE TO ME?

"This book is for action and not for discussion," said Aristotle of one of his works.

So is the Bible.

Discussion and understanding of the Bible is important, of course; but without action on the truth that emerges from its pages man is still without hope. The Word of God must constantly be applied in the life of the believer through the assistance of the Holy Spirit, for that is the only way to grow.

The Spirit who gave the Scripture in the first place has the ministry of helping the Christian to grasp the truth of the Scriptures.

Thus the Bible is the light on the path that leads to eternal life, and God's Spirit is the Guide.

So, follow on.

Handbook for Life

Imagine this scene before the Water Gate in Jerusalem. People everywhere, pressing in from all sides, and waiting quietly. Wall-to-wall people, eager to hear the reading of the Book.

The people had been through rough times. Long ago they had turned away from the Lord, and from the reading of the Law. Their spiritual life had been in serious decline. As a nation they had gone into captivity. However, Ezra the scribe had returned to Jesusalem 13 years before this and had begun to emphasize the importance of turning back to the Lord.

Now the people were open. They too were eager for the reading of the Word. So the great congregation, both of men and women, stood there for the entire morning, listening attentively to the books of the Law being read.

"So they read in the book in the law of God distinctly, and gave the sense, and caused them to understand the reading" (Nehemiah 8:8).

This reading took place for seven days.

And the results were striking.

A revival swept through Jerusalem.

There was a great turning back to the Lord.

This discovery of the Word, and acceptance of it, led to a great awakening. Repentance was followed by fresh commitment to follow the purposes of God, and to fulfill the requirements of the law.

Discovery of the truths of God's Word is always refreshing. It leads to a new sense of life in fellowship with God, especially to those who recognize that God has provided a remedy for sin through His Son, Jesus Christ.

Whenever God's people give themselves to serious study and application of God's Word—as opposed to routine exposure to the Bible, without serious intentions to put it into action—the results will be the same. God honors His Word. He has given it for a purpose, and that purpose is to waken man to the presence of God in the world. When man turns his back on the Bible he turns his back on God. For The Word is the written revelation of God.

Commandments to Live By

Take your Bible.

Look at it closely.

Like any other book it is made of paper, ink, stitching, binding and covers. It has come from the printing press, the trimmer, the stitcher—much like any other volume.

But it is not like any other volume.

And it is not the physical making of it that has anything to do with the difference. Nor is it even in the brilliancy of the men who actually put their pen on the page.

It is the ultimate source of this message that makes this an extraordinary set of books—the Holy Bible, as it says on the spine.

God's Word.

God's message to all mankind.

"Then shall I not be ashamed, when I have respect unto all thy commandments," says the psalmist in Psalm 119:6.

The Bible deserves our obedience because it is God speaking to man. God has something to say. It is worth our listening to. Be available to hear Him out.

Perhaps the Bible has become commonplace to us because of its availability. It is the most available book in the world. This is in great contrast to earlier centuries when it was necessary for scribes to copy manuscripts letter by letter.

Popular availability of books was nonexistent in those times.

Today we have it available in scores of different translations. Nobody within our culture can say that he cannot get his hands on a Bible.

But, has it become too commonplace?

Not that there are too many Bibles in existence. But have we allowed ourselves to discount the value of the Word, just because it is easy to get?

We do not have to stand in the city square from early morning till noon in order to hear the reading of the Word as they did in Nehemiah's day. Do we recognize that right there on the night table beside our bed are God's commandments to live by?

So, Live, Christian, Live!

Cause for Rejoicing

"I have rejoiced in the way of thy testimonies, as much as in all riches" (Psalm 119:14).

That's a switch!

At least it would be within our materialistic society, which puts so much value on possessions, status symbols, the right address, the car in the driveway, the Ivy League school, even the right church to attend. Those are the things that give so many people satisfaction within our situation today.

And that may not be greatly different from other times in history. The distribution of wealth may have changed considerably, but the basic value system may be more like previous generations than we would imagine. The psalmist was suggesting that high value was set on riches even in his time. And it seems clear that he was in a good situation to make a comparison.

But he bursts out with this exclamation that he rejoices more in "the way of thy testimonies" than in riches.

Evidently the psalmist had wide experience. He knew what it was to have riches, and he knew what it was to follow the ways indicated in the testimonies, or the law, of the Lord.

There is a peculiar satisfaction that comes from knowing that one is walking in the ways that God has ordained. It is an inner delight, a sense of rejoicing. And it cannot be compared with the satisfactions that come from things and symbols and riches.

The rejoicing that comes from following the

Lord has a deeper quality to it, a more lasting satisfaction, a feeling of rightness.

Meditation is a lost art to modern man with all his riches, and his delight in material things. The rushing about of our times tends to shatter the possibilities and the actual opportunities for meditation. But there is value in it nevertheless. Meditation on God's Word, along with the application of it in daily life, leads to the rejoicing the psalmist describes.

Practical Instruction

People need people.

That is a basic fact of our human existence. Hermits are few. Even at that they are aberrations in our social system. There is something cuckoo about a hermit. People need the attention, love and concern of other people. Not to have it is a form of emotional starvation.

God meant people to love each other.

He saw that Adam was lonely, that he needed a mate—not just a slave, but a mate. This implies fellowship, consolation, encouragement, sympathy and mutual regard.

Regard is that human quality that shows consideration for other people. It sees them, hears them, appreciates them as real people, and not just as cardboard images moving across the stage of time. It is one form of love.

Do you slow down enough to see people? Have you the time to get involved in their hurts, and to help them face their problems? Are you willing to let them vent their feelings on you, and even then understand?

Are you willing to relinquish your own position in center stage in favor of someone else who wants some human recognition? Are you responsive to people, allowing them to feel that they are important?

All these things are a part of what is implied and suggested in Paul's beautiful essay on love in I Corinthians 13. And there is much more. Life is a constant round of interactions with other people. How we respond to them, how we indicate our regard for them as human beings—in spite of all the differences that there may be between us—is of the essence. Paul elevates it to the most important consideration in the Christian life.

This is practical.

It can be applied.

In fact, you will either live by this principle today, or you will choose to live unto yourself only. This is the only alternative. The choice which reflects God's love in Jesus Christ is a very clear one. Thus, to you, Christian, there is no alternative.

Correction from God

Paul was concerned.

It seems that Timothy had cooled off somewhat in his fervor for the Lord. Perhaps this was due to the fact that he had been removed for some time from direct fellowship with the apostle Paul.

It is a serious thing to be out of touch with other Christians. It can allow the devil an extra armlock on your life. The values of Christian fellowship are important, especially at the point when they get beyond formal contacts. Unfortunately many of our church contacts today are so formalized that they do not provide any real sense of Christian fellowship.

Without that fellowship things can cool off, as seemed to be the case with Timothy. And that was the reason for Paul's gentle rebuke in writing to Timothy. In fact, Paul implies more about Timothy's situation than he says directly.

Paul's words to Timothy are God's words to us. See II Timothy chapter 1. Which of us can say that he has not cooled off at some time in his love for Jesus Christ? Which of us can say that we are maintaining a consistent spiritual aliveness? And which of our churches can boast that it has not experienced the coolness that must have been true of Timothy?

The rebuke stands.

"So keep my words in your mind as the pattern of sound teaching, given to you in the faith and love of Christ Jesus. Take the greatest care of the good things which were entrusted to you by the Holy Spirit who lives within us" (II Timothy 1:13,14, Phillips).

The reminder is needed.

Spiritual Training Manual

Don't be surprised if you meet opposition. It is sure to come. The Christian life is never really free from it and it was not meant to be. Jesus made that clear.

But it is also true that the Christian is given the resources to meet the opposition.

It is something like the ball team going onto the field. There is just no doubt about the fact that there is going to be opposition. That is what the game is all about. It would be nonsense not to expect it.

But the question that follows is: What can be done to meet the opposition, and to be able to handle it?

For the ball team the answer is clear. Train. Build up muscle and coordination. Understand the plays. Know your own strength and know the strength of the other team. Those are the elements that make for a winning team. They make for confidence, which is another way of saying faith.

For the Christian the answer is equally clear. Train. Build up spiritual muscle. Keep feeding on God's Word, for energy and body-building strength. Follow the instructions of the Coach. Learn your strength, and the strength of the opposition.

It's much the same ball game.

But how many Christians take it even as seriously as the athletes who train for professional sports? "But," someone objects, "that is their life; that is the only thing that they have to do."

Yes, you'd better believe it is. If it isn't what they really live for they won't last long.

And should a commitment to Christ be anything less? Should it not be the thing to live for with every bit as much dedication as a professional ball-player, and indeed much more? Any Christian who is willing to face that question, and to answer it in the affirmative, brings himself to the place where God can use him in a wonderful way.

From there on the Word gives the answers on a day-to-day basis. It is a sort of guide both in training and in the contest on the field. The help of other Christians who have been through the struggle can be of great help too.

With this combination, and the coaching of the Holy Spirit, the opposition can be handled.

Revelation of Jesus Christ

"Turn away mine eyes from beholding vanity; and quicken thou me in thy way" (Psalm 119:37).

The frustration of being human is rooted in the fact that we exist in two worlds. Paul described this frustration in Romans 7:22–24. "For I delight in the law of God after the inward man: but I see another law in my members, warring against the law of my mind, and bringing me into captivity to the law of sin which is in my members. O wretched man that I am! who shall deliver me from the body of this death?"

What torture!

Yet which of us has not experienced the struggle that Paul described? We are all too familiar with it.

But can it be resolved?

Paul, for his part, seems to sigh with relief, and he thanks God that the resolution of the problem is found in Jesus Christ. And he goes on to point out that there is no condemnation to them which are in Christ Jesus, for the law of life in Christ has made us free from the law that identifies sin and condemns to death.

There is a parallel between Paul's wrestlings and the psalmist's prayer that his eyes be turned away from beholding vanity. This world system in which we all have our physical existence has its own values, and without any connection to the higher order of spiritual values everything turns out to be nothing.

Yes, everything is nothing—without a relationship to God.

And that relationship is only possible through the Word. God made His Word personal in Jesus Christ. And He perpetuated it for our benefit in written form, the Bible. Thus the psalmist and Paul are basically saying the same thing—that release from frustration and vanity is in the Word. It is in the written Word that we meet the person of Jesus Christ. He frees us from the binding, condemning effect of the Law, and by the Holy Spirit He empowers us to walk in His way.

He gives us life!

He frees us to serve God!

That is the abundant life which Jesus Christ promised. That's living!

Guidebook for Living

Nobody would set out on his first cross-country trip without consulting a map. The pilot must consult his maps in order to decide on his flight plan.

Likewise it is essential that any Christian wanting to live the Christian life consistently consult the map.

Our map is the Bible.

We will either use it or go astray.

Decide to use your Bible in at least three ways: (1) in daily personal fellowship with God; (2) in small group Bible study, fellowship and prayer; and (3) in larger group study, or formal Bible study.

You will find the going much better when you consult the map.

CHAPTER 6

HOW DO I PRAY?

The spiritual strength of the church, at any given time or place in history, is in direct relation to the spiritual strength of the members who make up the believing community.

It follows then that the church can be strengthened as the members within it are strengthened.

But how does that come about? Does it just happen?

Not likely.

Even in matters of spiritual growth, things don't just happen. There are certain rules to follow if growth is to be the outcome.

One major element in spiritual growth is prayer. In fact, it can be said flatly that without an effective prayer life it is quite impossible to be spiritually strong, or to grow in Jesus Christ.

To Whom Am I Speaking?

Few biblical personages can compare with Daniel in strength of character. He proved himself wise, daring and courageous on many occasions.

Even more important was Daniel's sense of God. It is impossible to read of his adventures without realizing that he was on intimate terms with God at all times, under all sorts of pressures.

As we shall see from a number of biblical passages, prayer is directly related to a strong sense of God—recognition of Him as both the Creator and Sustainer of the universe, Lord over heaven and earth.

Without this sense of God prayer will have little meaning. "He that cometh to God must believe that he is, and that he is a rewarder of them that diligently seek him" (Hebrews 11:6). This is basic to Christian faith.

If prayer has become a dreary exercise in your life, you might check your sense of God. Is He real to you? Do you see this world as the place where He has put you, in order to serve Him? If you have allowed God to become a sort of vague, general presence behind the world someplace—a point of theology, but not an everyday reality, then this is the place to begin. Take a note from Daniel's experience. Believe in God with everything you are, and everything you've got. Let the rest of your world shape up around Him.

Daniel and God had a two-way relationship. It was with God's help that Daniel had survived in office through several administrations. He was evidently recognized as a sort of international figure, because of his wisdom—the wisdom God had given him.

For God's part, He had found in Daniel a man whom He could trust with tremendous responsibility, and through whom He could help preserve the cause of His own people who were being held in captivity.

In a sense, it can be said that Daniel trusted God, and God in turn trusted Daniel. As you read Daniel 6 you can see why. In spite of a jealously motivated and cunningly devised conspiracy to undercut his office, Daniel was determined to follow through in his usual manner of petitioning God for His assistance in the matters of the day.

In Daniel 6:16 we can see that Daniel's faith was catching, even in the case of a pagan, vainglorious ruler. Anyone whose sense of God and the reality of prayer is genuine will have great influence on others around him.

It's Serious Business

Prayer can be regarded as a learned activity. It is not just a spontaneous unstructured response to the recognition of our need. As Jesus made very clear from his model prayer in Luke 11:2–4 prayer has a basic structure.

This does not mean that we must go to written prayers. We don't always need literary gems through which to petition the Almighty. But there is a natural approach to God in prayer.

Prayer should begin with an explicit recognition of who God is. The great I AM. The Alpha and the Omega from all eternity and all time. Yet we are also invited to approach Him on such intimate terms as "Father." What a vast, heart-expanding idea that is! The God of all creation is my Father.

Hallow His name! Utter it in holy tones!

May His rule over all be hastened!

Make all that He wills a reality on earth, as it is in heaven!

Lord, here is my life again today. Make it thy instrument of blessing.

These are implicit attitudes in the approach to God outlined in Jesus' model prayer.

To anyone who really believes in God, and in what the Scriptures have to say about Him, prayer is the most utterly logical thing in the world. In prayer, the heart opens up toward God like the blossom to the morning sun. It is a natural response to the light.

That is logic. But not always our experience.

Experience indicates something different. There is something about the processes of this world that seems to convince us that it is running completely on its own. The system seems to work without God. So we tend to go about our day's activities figuring everything quite apart from the will and purpose of God.

But it was not so with Jesus. He prayed. And if Jesus found prayer necessary, what can be said of the rest of us? Without it how can life be in line with God's purposes? Things get gummed up when we leave God out of life and become prayerless.

God wants us to throw ourselves into prayer with full seriousness, with all the insistence of the friend who has a real need. When God knows that your petitions are serious and felt deeply, He is usually ready to answer.

What About My Attitude?

Prayer fits into a whole complex of mutually supporting attitudes. These attitudes help hold each other up. One leads to another, until eventually they permeate the life. That is the ideal, and it works as long as we keep ourselves constantly open in God's direction. See Philippians 4:4–9.

It is interesting how growth takes place. As we go to God in prayer, He provides the spiritual cells which move in and improve, replace and extend the spiritual tissue. This takes place spiritually much the same as it does physically.

In Philippians, notice the importance of outlook. Anyone who is really in fellowship with God develops a certain outlook. When God is in the picture it has got to make a difference—a big difference! So if things don't look this way, if gloom has settled in, if you are depressed, always go back to checking your current relationship with God.

But don't believe for a moment that this means a flower-strewn-pathway sort of existence. Far from it! That certainly wasn't Paul's experience.

Do you remember Paul's experiences in Philippi?

He spent part of his time in the town prison. Then he was hustled out of town before more trouble could arise. His life was anything but calm, cool and collected. Yet through it all he testified of the peace and joy of the Lord. Now he was counseling the Philippians to share this same experience.

This positive outlook—the look at life that sees God in the picture—is a Christian characteristic. Whenever it is missing among Christians the church will be weak. When it is present, rejoicing and prayer and peace and the other attributes of the Christian are possible.

Peace, as a Christian characteristic, is especially important today. Life in our terribly complex world is structured to leave peace out. Yet it is under these conditions that Christian peace can be a testimony in itself. The Christian who sees God in control of every situation doesn't panic.

In fact, "panic-button Christians" are somehow out of alignment. We need to see God in the picture at all times, especially in the problems.

It's Hard Work

Prayer is not only a source of Christian character. It is also a test of it. It was for Daniel. And it was for Jesus. Think of the agonizing prayer that He went through in the Garden of Gethsemane.

Prayer is not a rosy little exercise to get the day off to a good start, or a sigh of relief that the day is over. At times it is the kind of wrestling match that Jacob went through. It is not always easy. It can be work.

In fact, prayer is the kind of work that tests the spiritual muscles. Like any program of exercise it must be kept up consistently. So Paul says: "Pray without ceasing." It is not enough to throw in a little prayer here and there. It must become a part of life—an approach to living that comes as naturally as breathing.

One of the troublesome things about this subject is that prayer is all too often regarded as an exercise of the pious. Real men, with ability to face all the problems of life, sometimes feel that there is an element of weakness in prayer. This is deception, and requires some further thinking in order to spot its fault.

In some ways, self-reliance is a commendable trait. It is a mark of maturity. The child puts away dependence on his parents and moves out on "his own," as it were, to face his own problems in life and to provide for his own needs. This is healthy.

But it would be wrong to picture him as totally independent. He is constantly dependent on the society around him. He must relate to society—contributing to it at times and drawing from it at other times. This dependence is natural. It is not a sign of weakness.

When a man marries he sets up a system of interdependence between himself and his wife. They rely on each other and contribute to each other's well-being. This dependence is not weakness.

It comes down to a matter of relationships. Prayer too involves relationships. It is a two-way affair. We render praise, glory, honor, reverence and thanksgiving to God—just because of who He is.

God in turn contributes to our spiritual growth and well-being as we fellowship with Him in prayer.

Prayer, therefore, is not a sign of weakness. It is the route to a meaningful and rewarding relationship to God.

The Lord Still Knows Best

Many biblical characters were tested severely. And their testing was frequently related to prayer. Daniel had to face an edict from the king not to pray. Paul was tested through unanswered prayer when he asked that his thorn in the flesh be removed. But God had a better plan and told Paul: "My strength is made perfect in weakness" (II Corinthians 12:9).

We find in Job the ultimate test of a man's character. God had withdrawn, and Job could not confront Him to be vindicated. But Job remained faithful to God, even when he felt that God had abandoned him.

It is fairly easy to put on a proper display in public, when everyone is watching your behavior. Especially in church life, it is easy to be fairly upright in character. Prayer may come easy, as a part of expected behavior. But when a person is in another setting, with other friends who have different standards, he may be quite another person.

And what is that same person when nobody is around? And what would he be if even God were not around? This is the ultimate test, and Job met it head on. He said: "Though he slay me, yet will I trust in him: but I will maintain my own ways before him" (Job 13:15).

One indicator of Job's real character was his reaction to his situation. Many a man would have followed his wife's advice to curse God and die. But Job was made of better stuff. In spite of all the pressures—loss of family, lands, flocks, home, wealth and even his own health—Job had a deep yearning for God. He maintained his belief that God had some purpose, some plan within which all of his experience would make sense.

In other words, he did not try to interpret God's character in light of his experience. It was the other way around. He let the whole matter be interpreted in the light of God's unquestionable goodness. That is why he could pray amid all his pain and loss.

Sickness, bereavement, financial loss and other problems are often the means of keeping people from God. They feel that God has let them down. They cannot pray. This betrays spiritual weakness.

If, like Job, we see that God is good no matter what happens to us, then there is always an openness in God's direction. And that openness is the key to effective prayer.

Keep in mind that Job saw the whole picture change later. God gave him more than he had in the beginning. Yet, in another sense, Job found he had everything even when he had nothing.

Not "Me First, God"

One point is essential in maintaining a healthy

prayer life. Make sure your prayers are not all self-centered.

Whenever prayer becomes highly self-centered it is a clue that a problem has arisen. Instead of making ourselves available to God, so that He can work through us, we have got it backwards. We are really trying to fit God into our plans and our way of life. Thus we can misunderstand prayer as something through which we get things for ourselves. Although it sometimes has that result, that is not the real purpose of prayer.

Paul appeals to Timothy to have the Christian community be broad in its prayer life. In fact, they should be broad enough to include "all men." Those who have political authority and governmental responsibility are to be included, in order that there could be peace for the Christian community to give its witness.

Paul's outlook and his prayers were shaped by his compulsion to declare to the world that God has provided for man's need in the person of Jesus Christ. Paul could never forget the role to which he was appointed by God—preacher, apostle and teacher of the Gentiles.

In his missionary outreach Paul depended on the prayers of other Christians as his major support. But Paul himself was broad in his outlook. He did not ask for prayer for himself alone, but seemed to be asking rather that the Christian community involve itself with the total process of Christian outreach to the world.

The reason for Paul's compulsion to proclaim the gospel is given in I Timothy 2:1–9. God is desirous

71

that all men should be reconciled to Him, but there is just one Mediator. Jesus Christ is the sole means of salvation. His death and resurrection are the only means by which man can be reconciled to God. This was the reason for Paul's determination to reach out to the whole world with the good news.

We need to ask ourselves whether the church today has maintained this view of its mission in the world. Paul found it welling up in his soul as something he was quite unable to resist. He said: "For though I preach the gospel, I have nothing to glory of: for necessity is laid unto me; yea, woe is unto me, if I preach not the gospel!" (I Corinthians 9:16).

Once we have that attitude, prayer will come quite naturally.

I Need to Pray to Live

Our very humanity calls us to pray! Weakness is our lot, especially when compared to the vastness of the universe in which we are placed. We cannot escape the recognition that the forces around us are really too great for us.

Whether we look at the heavens with the naked eye or probe them with a powerful telescope, we must stand back in awe at the vastness of space around us. So the psalmist asks: "What is man, that thou art mindful of him? and the son of man, that thou visitest him?" (Psalm 8:4). It is a good question. The answer remains forever a mystery. Yet the fact is that God desires man's fellowship.

Isaiah understood man's disposition to forget God. Through the prophet, God spoke to His people and cut their rationalizations to shreds. In effect, God asked: "How come you think your actions are hidden to Me? How can you suppose that I am off someplace doing something else, or looking the other way?" (See Isaiah 40:25–31.)

How often that is our reaction to God! Because we cannot perceive Him with the physical senses which we usually rely on, we conclude that God is not around. He is off somewhere doing something else. We would never admit this in theory, but we give plenty of evidence in our actions that this is really the way we think.

Yet God is still ready and waiting to respond when we call. He promises power to the faint, and strength to those who are weak. He delights in our fellowship and is ready to respond when we pour out our needs.

It is ridiculous to forget God—to leave Him out of the equation of life. Whenever we do, the real meaning in life is gone. We can go romping after temporary values, but they soon turn to dust. The only things really worth living for are rooted in God.

If we take that as a fact, life takes on new meaning. Every day becomes a new adventure with God. Problems are simply challenges to see God work, and prayer is the means by which we invite Him into each problem situation. Good things that come our way become fresh reasons to turn to God in thankfulness for all that He has done for us—and what He is doing in us.

Prayer, in short, depends entirely on an outlook that takes God for who He is.

In today's world, the home is usually considered a "secular" setting. We tend to associate any spiritual activity with the church, especially the sanctuary. Yet in the early period of Christianity there was no such thing as a church building. The home was used for prayer and worship.

In today's setting the prayer group in the home can be a strong support to the total program of worship and prayer which includes time spent in the church sanctuary.

Are you using your home for prayer, Bible study or evangelism? If not, begin now. Decide which of your neighbors might join you for an hour. Then decide what you might do to help them become better acquainted with Jesus Christ. And be sure to pray that God will make it real.

CHAPTER 7

HOW CAN I FIGHT
WHAT I CAN'T SEE?

"We are at war! It has just been announced."

A speaker had arrived somewhat late for a speaking engagement, and said that he had just been listening to his radio. Then he broke the terrible news that the nation was at war.

One woman screamed: "Oh, no! My son!"

Others almost fainted.

Throughout the entire audience there was a shiver. People leaned forward in their seats. Audible moans could be heard throughout the entire gathering.

That is the effect of one word: War. It is serious. It means a life and death struggle.

And it is not a coincidence that the Christian life is often described as warfare. It is meant to be that kind of thing—a serious, life and death matter.

Peace for the Soldier

It's too much.

Nobody can really take the words of Jesus at face value . . . can they?

Did He really mean it? Take no thought for the basic necessities of life; what we eat; what we are to drink, what we are to wear. These are essentials. We want to reply, "But if we don't think about these things, we won't be here to think about anything." See Matthew 6:25–34.

And what about Jesus' comparison between ourselves and the birds of the air, or the flowers of the field. They are just birds. Or just flowers.

It may be true that God has provided a system on which they can survive, without worrying about their survival, but . . .

Finally, our objections come to a grinding halt. There it is. There's the answer to it. At the root of it all we find the provision of God.

Just think how much the people of this world spend their time running after things which they consider the "necessities" of life. In addition to the essentials mentioned here, we now include education, transportation, housing, insurance (life insurance, health insurance, car insurance, income insurance, disability insurance, and all the other kinds), radios, television, lighting, plumbing, refrigeration, cooking appliances and then, of course, heating and air conditioning.

The bills pile up. And when the pay check comes we pass most of it along to provide for the many "necessities" of our existence. Now we must go back to work next week to keep the wolf from the door.

So we tromp the old treadmill.

Life must go on, we tell ourselves.

But then comes Jesus, with His suggestion that all these things will be provided for us, if . . .

If . . .

If we seek first the kingdom of God and His righteousness.

Just as flat as that.

For that is where the meaning in life begins. Without God, without His love in Jesus Christ, without His provision for us we don't have the things we really need anyway. So it begins right there.

And to the person who has "tried God" as it were, everything else does have its way of working out.

No sweat!

Not the Life for Weaklings

Who in the world would choose a tough route? Everybody is looking for an easy way.

Try the "good life." Take Broadway. Live it up.

That's the way people are today—and it's been that way for a long while.

But here stands a figure in history, Jesus Christ. And He says: "Don't take the easy way. It's not worth it. It leads to damnation. Be among the few who take the narrow road that leads to life." See Matthew 7:12–20.

And who will listen?

Jesus actually calls people to do what is not easy. The way is hard, because it constantly involves self-sacrifice. It seems so much more natural for us to run after self-expression and self-gratification. That is human nature in its fallen condition. And Jesus came to set man on another course—the course to life.

So, if we follow Jesus, we choose struggle.

That is why the gospel is "bad news," as someone has put it.

But that is not the end of the matter, fortunately. The narrow road does lead to life, and to fulfillment. In fact, it is the only life that is real in the long run. The broad road is temporal, and leads to destruction.

If this seems like a riddle, it's because it was meant to be that way. Not everybody catches on. Just a few really get it. But those few have something that is really worth having—life.

And they have found it by subordinating everything to the desire for God and for the bringing of His will to pass on earth. The whole texture of life has taken on a new feeling of reality to them.

In many ways they may look and act like other people. But they are not. They are on another road.

And their road is marked "true reality this way."

Too mystical?

Perhaps. But not to the person who has got his feet on that road. Then it is all very clear. Things somehow clear up when you get on the way.

And how do you find the way?

Well, there was One who said: "I am the way."

Proceed with Caution

Only a nut or a reckless maniac would boast about a list like the one in II Corinthians 11:23–33.

But then there's Paul, and the viewpoint of the person who has sold out so completely to God that nothing matters—whether it's pain or punishment, trouble or threats, pressure or peril, weariness or hunger, beatings or a thousand problems.

In fact, they all add up to glory. That's how Paul looked at it.

And that outlook is Christian.

It may not be very common, but yes, it *is* Christian.

Did Paul enjoy pain? Did he invite trouble? Did he want to die? Was he aiming for martyrdom? No. This is clearly not the case, from the record in verse 33—his humiliating means of escape from Damascus where the garrison of the governor wanted to apprehend him. Paul was human, and his feelings and reactions must have been much like our own.

Any difference we may notice was due to the fact that Paul had arrived at the place where he could say: "But none of these things move me, neither count I my life dear unto myself, so that I might finish my course with joy, and the ministry, which I have received of the Lord Jesus, to testify the gospel of the grace of God" (Acts 20:24).

That was his whole outlook. To serve God was really what mattered.

So Paul says in II Corinthians 11:28 that his attention was not on the problems but rather on the care of the churches which God had committed to him. That was what really concerned him. And there is good evidence of that in the number of letters which he wrote in order to assure the health and the growth of the churches.

It is evident in this letter that Paul was embarrassed about one point. He had to submit again his credentials as an apostle of Jesus Christ. His authority had been challenged by some of the Corinthians.

So, if it comes down to that, Paul says, I will tell you what I have been through for the sake of the gospel—these troubles are my credentials.

And indeed they were. What other person would go through so many problems except one who had been commissioned on the Highest Authority.

Power to Survive

Weakness and strength. Opposites.

Either you are weak or you are strong. You cannot be both. Right?

Wrong.

Here's a man who says: "When I am weak, then am I strong" (II Corinthians 12:10).

Nonsense?

Not exactly. If you follow the reasoning that leads to it, it makes great sense. The trick is being able to follow that logic—God's logic.

The sense of it all is quite impossible unless you have God in the picture. You must let everything center around the fact that God is at the heart of this equation. Then it begins to make sense.

It is something like a person out swimming in the ocean, who is caught in the riptide. It pulls him farther and farther out to sea. He begins to struggle against the current. But he is quite helpless to overcome it. Then he becomes frantic.

From the shore, a lifeguard dives into the surf and swims out to the victim. He shouts: "Take it easy; don't fight it." This is against all the natural instincts of the victim. He wants to fight the current, but the lifeguard instructs him to relax.

The life of the victim might well depend on his ability to follow instructions. If he struggles at all he will be struggling against the efforts of the lifeguard to save him. His life depends on giving up to the strength of the lifeguard, who has more reserve strength and greater swimming capability.

The Christian must begin with God on just that arrangement, for he cannot save himself. God alone has the power to save.

But it does not stop there.

The Christian must continue to rest in God's superior power, and trust that His power will replace the weakness that characterizes all human effort, even the best.

Dependency on God is the clue.

Our weakness *is* His strength.

Wisdom to Survive

"If any of you lack wisdom, let him ask . . ."
(James 1:5).

How often this verse is used in a general way to
petition for wisdom in making some decision or
other. Or even more generally it is used as the basis
of a request for overall wisdom—as if this verse
might be the short-cut to sagacity.

While God is undoubtedly more pleased to have
us be wise rather than foolish, the verse does not
mean exactly what those petitions imply.

James is speaking within a certain context here,
and his suggestion that wisdom is available refers
to a particular sort of wisdom. It is the wisdom that
is from above (3:17). James suggests that this wisdom is reflected in good conversation and meek-
ness (3:13), and that it is very different from the
self-conscious, self-centered sort of wisdom which
he says is "devilish" (3:15).

With that distinction in mind then James says
there is a God-given wisdom (1:5), and the person
who has it will also have the other characteristics
that he goes on to mention in his letter.

Notice the practicality of James. He keeps his
eye on the ball. He is conscious of the day-to-day
mode of living of the Christian. Anyone who genuinely accepts God's wisdom—the outlook that
comes from receiving God's grace in Jesus Christ—

will have a distinctive way of life. And it must be free from contradictions.

No double standards. No double vision. No double mindedness.

That is what results from accepting Christ, but not letting Him affect your life too much. Thus we have Christians who try to commute between the kind of life Jesus lived and a way of life geared to the usual standards of the world around us.

It doesn't add up, James says.

The Lord levels all distinctions. Social status loses all its meaning in the church. Wealth and honor and titles are left outside. Race and riches make no difference whatever. The things that count are the things that reflect the love of God and the works of righteousness.

Stand, Soldier

Apostasy has drawn stern warnings from the author of the letter to the Hebrews. Judgment and fiery indignation are in store for those who turn away from God's grace. The Lord will judge His people. It is a fearful thing to fall into the hands of the living God. See Hebrews 10:31–39.

But . . .

The author of Hebrews turns to a brighter thought. He asks these Christians to remember earlier days in their faith when, having found the light in Jesus Christ, they endured "a great fight of afflictions."

They were under fire, and they were able to stand. This serves as a solid testimony of their genuine devotion to Christ. Their lives were consistent with the light they had been given.

In fact, these people had somehow been made a spectacle to the world because of their faith in Jesus Christ. It was like being displayed in the arena, where everyone could see them, taunt them, reproach them, and afflict them.

What was more, they had associated with those who had the reputation of being Christians. That was a very unpopular, perhaps dangerous, association. Yet they were true, because of their patience in the faith.

And evidently one of those with whom these Christians were associated, unashamedly, was the author of Hebrews himself.

It takes a certain sort of character to be a Christian. Or perhaps it would be better to say that Christian faith, if it is really applied, builds a certain sort of character into the believer.

Fidelity is one of the characteristics.

Patience is another.

We have need of patience, we are told in verse 36, so that after we have done the will of God, we shall not give up before seeing Christ at His return, and receiving our reward.

We don't usually see the full results of our service to Jesus Christ. If we see anything at all it is no more than a small part of what we might really accomplish for Him. It takes time, and a great deal more insight than any of us has to trace the exact effects of our actions in directing people toward Christ.

So that is where patience comes in. We need it to

keep us on the track toward the goal, even though we may not see the full results of our actions.

The Long View

Take the long view.

It's the only way to go, if you want to live joyfully, peacefully, effectively.

Life is filled with immediacies. This thing or that has to be done—now! And it does. So many things need doing now. They are important.

But we become victim to these immediate problems so easily. They get us down. We are captive to them without realizing it.

Mentally, spiritually, we need to be able to back off and take the long view. We need to see what's ahead—not just the problems of today, the activities of this afternoon and this evening, or even next month or next year.

We need to see further than that.

We can look forward, Peter suggests in the first chapter of his first epistle, to the denouement of history. And we see ourselves in it—for God has reserved us a place, and it will be revealed when the curtain of history is pulled back and we see things as they really are. That is the hope, the long view, of the Christian.

And it helps us—or it should—in handling these pesky immediacies (and the huge problems too) that encumber us in our here-and-now existence.

This is not escapism.

The attitude of the escapist—and some Christians are guilty of this—is one that substitutes the long view, the hope in Christ's return, for current responsibility. This was never intended to be the Christian's attitude. It is irresponsible. The Christian is not an escapist from the problems of life.

On the contrary, he faces the problems of life with a certain relish. He knows that his final salvation from the problems of this world is assured, but in the meantime he faces them with all the fortitude that the Holy Spirit provides. No matter how great the problem, how severe the trial, it is not too great for God. It is something that can be handled, because God is our partner in handling it.

That is the Christian view of things.

That is the source of strength in life.

That is the hope, joy and peace of the Christian.

So, Peter says, take the long view of things. Keep your eye on more than the problems of the moment. The result will be greater capability to handle those problems, for you are not their victim after all. They are your opportunity to face life in the strength of God.

It's a Struggle

Struggle.

By itself it stands as an ugly word. But throughout this chapter we have met the word in many places, and we have seen it under new light.

Now we must put these ideas into work clothes. We can face the struggle in a strength that the world apart from Christ cannot share.

Determine to face your problems in God's strength—and then delight in watching Him work.

CHAPTER 8

DO I LIKE TO BE NEAR GOD?

Nobody has seen God at any time.

Those who are without God have no hope in this world or any other.

But God is love. And God wants men's fellowship and worship.

At first the above facts do not seem to square off with each other. How can a loving God who cannot be seen insist that men should know Him, and fellowship with Him and worship Him?

The only satisfactory way in which we can know God is in the person of His Son, Jesus Christ. Man's deepest desires for God, and God's longing for man's fellowship find their fulfillment in the reconciliation provided in Christ.

Knowing that, worship should be the natural response of the believing heart.

Sometimes I Like to Be Near

There are certain times when the heart really thrills to being in the presence of a particular person. Frequently this is the experience of the young person in love.

Just to be "on the street where you live," has all sorts of romantic and thrilling side effects, as the song by that name suggests. The feet of the romantic young man hardly touch the ground, all because he is in the vicinity of the one he loves.

There are times when we may have the same feeling about God. We are thrilled by Him. Just to sense His presence is to see the whole world with other eyes. Everything else takes on a new perspective when we have Him fixed in our consciousness, and when we want to be with Him.

This is the experience of the psalmist in Psalm 95. He delights at the very idea of being in the presence of the Lord. The thought of God's majestic greatness has drawn out his spirit in worship. Singing, joyful noises, thanksgiving and worship are the result.

It is quite possible to get up in the morning with that sort of spirit—and to have it remain until you lie down to sleep at night. This does not mean that everything in between will be easy. And it does not mean that the sense of worship is nothing more than a generally good feeling about life.

88

It means simply that the recognition of God brings a natural response from the soul—at least it will if you let it. The soul that opens up in the direction of God is doing what it was made to do.

The thing that so often cuts us off from this attitude is the pressure of this world to fit into its mold —its thought patterns and frame of reference. They so often seem structured to leave God out. And they come so naturally to us. When we follow them, leaving God out of the picture, we soon find that our delight at His presence is missing.

Whenever that happens, it is time to join the psalmist in reminding ourselves who God is, and what He expects of us.

And remember that God is always open to us in Jesus Christ. He said: "I am the way . . . no man cometh unto the Father, but by me" (John 14:6).

I Talk to God

Do you ever suspect that certain prayers are not real? God must have that suspicion concerning a great many prayers that are thrown in His direction.

Perhaps you are listening to a public prayer. Or worse still, perhaps you are offering a public prayer. And suddenly you have that feeling that the prayer is offered more with the intent of impressing men than with reaching God. If that is what is really going on, it isn't prayer at all.

That is why Jesus was so emphatic that His followers should exercise care about giving money or prayers or sacrifices in public. It is too easy to get caught up in the wrong motivation. Religious "status-climbing" takes over, and the result is the cancelling out of the validity of the prayers or gifts offered with that in mind.

It is interesting that those who have often been most effective in doing things for God have been men and women whose prayers were very simple. George Müller, the prayer warrior of Bristol, England, was said to offer extremely simple, direct prayers. It was as if he were simply in conversation with God—which he was.

A certain amount of healthy self-examination is always necessary in the Christian life. In this connection we always need to ask ourselves: What is it that makes me give? And what is it that makes me pray?

If the clear answer to this is simply that we see God for who He is, and want therefore to give back to Him all that we are, then we are on strong ground. The trouble is that all too often that is not the simple, true answer. The facts may be that we are really involved in trying to impress other people. And that is never good—even when we feel that we have the "right" people in mind. We must have a mind to seek God, and "impress" Him—which is only possible through Jesus Christ.

Another fallacy is the feeling that God answers long prayers. There may be good reason for "all night prayer meetings" but it is not to be found in the argument that we will be heard for our much speaking. The answer is more likely to be that the simple exercise of getting apart with God at an unusual time may be the means through which we arrive at a really prayerful attitude in our own lives.

In prayer, in giving, in worship it is important to make sure that God is the real focus of the soul's attention.

I Love Him

Since God knows what we have need of even before we ask, what is the use of asking? The question is a good one, because the only sensible answer to it brings us right back to the basics.

More than anything else, God is interested in a relationship with us. For some strange, wonderful reason He is in love with us. In fact, He loved us so much that He gave His Son as the sacrifice for our sins.

It is one thing to say that God really *loves* me—but it is another thing to grasp it. When you do, all life should take shape around it.

The late theologian, Karl Barth, was once asked by reporters what was the most profound thought that had ever gone through his mind. After pausing only a moment Barth responded:

"Jesus loves me; this I know,
For the Bible tells me so."

God not only provided for our spiritual needs in Jesus Christ, but He also is interested in our material needs.

"But," our persistent questioner asks, "if God loves us, and knows our needs before we pray, why doesn't He supply the need and forget about the prayer?"

It is often our needs that bring us to God. In many cases they are the means of literally driving us back to God. We rediscover our need of Him, and consequently we again find ourselves in fellowship with Him.

Before we pour out our needs to God, as Jesus suggests in The Lord's Prayer, it is appropriate that we bring the Father our praise and thanksgiving. Only after we establish fellowship with God is it appropriate that we recite all our needs.

This puts things in perspective again. We must always be careful that prayer does not become a means of fitting God into our lives, but rather of making our lives bring honor and glory to God. When we get these things in the right order, we will be in a much better position to see our prayers answered.

And even if they should not be answered in the way we expect, a more important thing has happened—if we have been in real fellowship with God.

God Needs Me

The Bible really has something for everybody, and for every situation. God thought of everything, it seems, when He gave the Word.

In John 4 Jesus is at a well in Samaria, during the heat of the day. And He is in conversation with a woman of the streets from the nearby town.

Yet Jesus was perfectly willing to talk with her. More so than most of us would be under similar circumstances. Social usages are all too often our only guide. We see people only as our society sees them—and for that reason we are all too often caught in the web of unwitting discrimination.

Not Jesus. He saw people as they really were. And often the outcasts were His point of contact with society, while the respectable and self-righteous were much harder for Him to reach.

When the woman sensed that she was talking to a prophet (not yet understanding that He was in fact the Messiah) she brought up a major point of contention between the Jews and the Samaritans. She pointed out the difference in belief relating to the proper place of worship.

Jesus was prepared for the question. He pointed out that the Jews had been the recipients of the revelation of God's truth—the Scriptures of the Old Testament. It was on the basis of that revelation, and from among the Jews that God brought forth His plan of salvation. Jesus, the Son of God, was a Jew.

But in answering her question more directly Jesus pointed out that the time was coming when worship would not be a matter of place, but rather of genuine openness to God. This was what He had come to make possible. That is why He could say: "The hour cometh, *and now is,* when the true worshipers shall worship the Father in spirit and in truth" (John 4:23).

Notice too that Jesus says clearly that the Father's desire is to have such people to worship Him. Here it is, stated as plainly as possible. God wants a relationship—of respect, of dependency and of intimate fellowship—with people, whether an outcast or a head of state. The essence of real life is in responding to God's desire at that point.

In the Presence of God

There is something of a mystery in the vision which Isaiah recorded in Isaiah 6. From the description we might gather that he had gone to the Temple and that this vision took place somewhere in the Temple area.

If this was so, how many others might have been present? Anyone? And if there were others present did they see what Isaiah saw? Or was there some dimension of the scene that was visible only to him, while others were quite blind to it? Or could it be that Isaiah was given this vision in some other place entirely?

We don't know. But there is no record of anyone else being present and seeing what Isaiah saw. In other words, God seemed specially intent on getting through to Isaiah on this occasion. He had a plan that related to the future and to His chosen people. And Isaiah figured into that plan.

God's total plan is large enough to include every one of us. He desires to have us meet Him, to see ourselves, to find His forgiveness and then to discover where we fit into His plan.

Isaiah knew that God was interested in the people around him. In fact, Isaiah identified so closely with his people that he felt their sins and even confessed their sins before God. It was then that the seraphim flew with the live coal, from off the altar, and touched his lips and promised him forgiveness.

Then comes the indication that God needed a man—one who could present His message to the people, even though most of them would not respond.

And Isaiah, having seen the Lord, responded eagerly. God's message for that time was not a very popular one, but that didn't slow Isaiah down. He was ready to fit in however God wanted.

Life reaches its highest meaning when a person fits into the slot God has for him, and when he accepts the work God has for him to do. Usually this turns out to be exactly the place where God has already placed you, except that it becomes a more meaningful place of service when you have seen the Lord.

Fellowship Together with God

Worship, as we know it in today's setting, is too apt to be anonymous. It was never intended to be that way.

It is possible to participate fully in some worship services without ever knowing the name of anyone in the congregation, except perhaps the minister and others listed in the bulletin.

Some people object that it should be that way. They don't want to go into a church service and be buttonholed by someone who is trying to steer them to all sorts of other activities. They would rather remain anonymous, and uninvolved.

That may be their desire, but it is not in line with the picture of what the church ought to be as it is given to us in the New Testament. Christian commitment demands involvement, first with God and then with His people—and indeed with all people, if you take God's love in its broadest sense.

But this is not a brief for buttonholing. That too is based on a misconception of the New Testament picture of Christian commitment and involvement. It is too superficial. It is so often geared just to activity, not to real people.

Wherever Jesus was, He was involved with people—with their outlook, their problems, their joys and sorrows, their needs and their loneliness. As He was always in touch with God, so He was always in touch with people around Him. And in that He set us an example.

But being in touch with God and men requires the sustaining contact of the inner circle—the close-in-group that helps build muscle in the things of the Spirit. This is discipleship at work. This is finding each other in Christ. This is the dimension in which worship and service are brought together.

This is how the author of the book of Hebrews envisioned it in chapter 10:19–25: a close fellowship, spurring each other to do good, and putting love into action, assembling regularly in the name of Christ, urging one another on, and thus upholding together common faith in Jesus Christ.

Individual believers? Yes, but joined together in corporate commitment, worship and service.

God of Glory

The entire Bible is a book of vivid images. But of all the books of the Bible, none can compare with the book of Revelation in the vividness of the visual imagery that it presents.

The biblical books which are prophetic in nature —such as Daniel, Ezekiel, the minor prophets and Revelation—tend to present the most intense visual displays. Scenes leap onto the mental screen as one reads. The reason for this seems to be the fact that God used visions to show the prophets things in their proper perspective, and things as they would come to pass in the future.

It is very human, and in that sense very natural, for us to attach a strong feeling of truth and rightness to things as we see them. But all of us are familiar with optical illusions. Sometimes things are not what they seem. All our senses seem to tell us one thing, but the facts turn out to be otherwise.

So it is in this world. There are some instances when things are not just what they might seem. For instance, it might seem natural to us to picture heaven as a sort of redecorated version of earth. But that does not do it justice. The description of heaven can hardly be contained in the terminology of earth. But if man is to know anything at all about heaven, it will have to be in earthly terms, for these are all he has.

Thus when God showed John things that were to come, the resulting visual images put into human terms often seem very strange to us. The deficiency is not one of God's revelation, but rather of man's ability to grasp things that are difficult for human comprehension.

To put it another way, heaven is a "far out" place. And anyone who is to really understand it will have to be pretty "far out" himself. That was John's experience, and he had the additional task of putting the things he saw in writing.

And what a result! In Revelation 4 we catch a view of the throne, and the creatures around the throne, and we hear the praise they sing, and we see twenty-four majestic personages casting down their crowns before the Lord in adoration.

What glory! What praise! What honor and power! This is the picture of the presence of the Lord, and note how much it corresponds to the scene described by Isaiah, when he saw the Lord in the Temple (Isaiah 6:1—8). It seems that Isaiah and John were tuned to the same channel, although they lived many centuries apart.

CHAPTER 9

DO I HAVE WHAT GOD WANTS?

Man has not learned to live until he has learned to give. Total self-centeredness is sin. And the opposite is outgoing love, actively interpreted in giving.

This is one key to understanding something about the nature and personality of God. In the heart of God was the desire to have someone with whom He could have fellowship—and to whom He could express His love. The drama of creation, the fall of man and man's redemption through Jesus Christ, is a story of God's outgoing love and His willingness to give His dearest possession in order to redeem man from sin, and to make a reinstatement to fellowship possible.

Thus, when man learns to give himself, he is following God's example.

He Wants Me, Alive

Look alive, here comes the undertaker!

Some people, if you judge by their sense of meaning in life, will hardly make it. It is a good thing the undertaker needs a death certificate! These people can hardly be called alive. They move through their mundane existence from day to day without purpose or direction. The only thing that keeps them going is the need to keep going. They are lost. Dead, even while they live.

Yet Jesus said: "I am come that they might have life, and that they might have it more abundantly" (John 10:10). Real living, purposeful existence, abundant life are to be found in Him. He is the beginning of living. Whoever is without Him is without a full and meaningful life.

Those who come to faith in Jesus Christ know this. Their experience verifies it. But it is also true that they need constantly to be reminded of it. For some reason, the human tendency is to settle back to the ordinry existence again. Because we are left in this human situation, and because we are constantly influenced by the world around us, the qualities of abundant living in Jesus Christ can be let to slip. It is necessary to keep ourselves on a constant refresher course if we are to keep on living the abundant life.

Paul undoubtedly has this fact in mind as he urges the Christians in Rome to become "living sacrifices" to God. (See Romans 12.) This is a voluntary thing. God will not *make* them do it. And Paul *cannot* make them do it. It has to be the full and complete surrender of themselves to God and His purposes.

Paul describes this as the rational thing for them to do. They must think about it, and their response must be a volitional one. They are either willing or unwilling to follow his advice. And the burden to take action is with them. Nobody can do it for them.

And *them* becomes *us*—for Paul is stating a principle that applies as much to us as it did to the Christians in Rome.

We soon learn that when we give ourselves to God, we give ourselves to others as well—especially to those who are already in the body of Christ. Our service to God is service to them. We aid growth as we give ourselves in whatever way God chooses.

He Wants My Trust

Giving ourselves may seem foolish. Perhaps that is just the point Paul is making to the Corinthians in his first letter to them. See I Corinthians 3:18. It is the foolish man who is wise, Paul says. Wisdom appears to be foolishness in God's book. And God is pictured as laying traps for the schemers.

So, which way is up?

How can you tell real wisdom from the phony?

Who is wise after all?

Should we despair of *all* human wisdom?

The only way of finding an answer to these questions—at least a satisfying answer—is to examine the context in which Paul is speaking, and to see clearly the contrast he is making.

Paul's focus is on the gospel, and on the process by which the believing community grows in its understanding of the gospel. He points out that the gospel which he has declared to these Christians is not his own. It is from God. The gospel is in no way, and never can be, a human invention or accomplishment.

Thus he describes the gospel as "hidden wisdom, which God ordained before the world unto our glory: which none of the princes of this world knew" (I Corinthians 2:7,8). Then Paul follows this by saying (in verses 12,13 of chapter 2) that this message was given by God, and is not a product of man's wisdom. Man naturally tends to reject the gospel—simply because it is not of his making, and he dislikes the implications of dependency which are inherent in the gospel.

In the first two verses of chapter 4, Paul explains his own role in declaring the gospel. He is the steward, or trustee, of something which has been given from the outside. And of course, the chief requirement of all trustees is that they be faithful in the execution of their intended role.

And Paul *was* faithful. Not because he wanted popular approval, but rather he desired God's approval.

Possession of the gospel brings responsibility—and accountability. The simple fact that we have it demands that we share it. We cannot be moral without sharing it. What would we say of any man who knew a cure to some serious disease and would not make it known if others would benefit by it?

If we are Christians, we must be accountable.

He Wants My Undivided Attention

Anyone who likes puzzles should like Paul's letters to the Corinthians. They are a series of paradoxes. They consist of contradictions. Things that cannot be, yet are. For example, see II Corinthians 4:7–18.

Essentially these statements grow out of Paul's ability to live in two worlds at the same time—without being a split personality. He begins by observing that we have this treasure—the knowledge of Jesus Christ—in "earthen vessels." In other words, this valuable commodity is held in earthen jars, which are ordinary and fragile.

Amazing. God allowed the golden commodity of the ages to be put in ordinary earthen jars. Why?

The answer is clear. In the long run, the very fact that the gospel was left for man to communicate proves the power of God. Human frailty gives all the more chance for failure, but it also makes all the more room for God to demonstrate His power. That too was a part of God's pre-planning.

Realizing this, and knowing that the whole plan is in the hands of God, Paul could not be discouraged or dissuaded in his mission. He was simply a servant doing his duty to the best of his ability.

Paul exemplified the character of a man who was indestructible, because he was looking always at God and not at the circumstances.

So when intense difficulties arose on every side, he was not distressed.

When circumstances were perplexing, he did not despair.

When he was persecuted, he did not feel forsaken.

When he was thrown to the ground and left for dead, he was not destroyed.

When his life was threatened, he remembered the resurrection of the Lord Jesus.

Paul considered all of these things trivial, because all of them could work to the glory of God, in whose service he was engaged. Thus he never fainted, or gave up in spirit. In fact, they could have destroyed Paul physically—and at times they tried—yet he somehow experienced that inner renewal which is common to those who walk so closely with God.

When you consider Paul's outlook here, the rapid expansion of the gospel through the early church becomes more understandable.

He Wants My Stewardship

It is always hard to give up the things we have earned. Whenever we work for something, it tends to become a part of us. Our labor is very much "us." And when we translate our labor, or our skill, or our knowledge, into material things we feel that they too are in some measure a part of us. Thus it is especially hard to give up anything which is so much attached to us.

That's the pocketbook test. Consider how difficult it is to give up our money. Yet that is one important way in which we demonstrate how much our earnings mean to us. It is put somewhere in our scale of values, and we contribute in proportion to what we are committed to. If we are really committed to Christ we will find ways in which we can contribute to the extension of His gospel and to the needs of others who follow Him.

In II Corinthians 9:6–15 Paul was discussing a relief fund which was to be applied to the needs of certain Christians who were in Jerusalem. He gives a considerable part of this epistle to encouraging these Christians in their liberality, and letting them know how the offering would be taken and the effect that it would have. He made it clear that he was asking other churches to participate also.

In making his appeal Paul reminded these Christians at Corinth that the real source of their own supply was in God. He speaks of God being able to make us abound in grace and in all good things.

It is terribly dangerous to set up any neat formulas whereby we expect to get back from God specific things in return for the things we give. Whenever that motivation enters the picture there is real question whether we are giving at all—at least in the spirit that God expected. We simply cannot bargain with God that way. He must always be Lord.

But it is still true that "we can never outgive

God." For one thing, we start so far behind we could never catch up. He gave His Son. We can never give anything in that measure. All we can give is everything, and that is all God wants. But we can also rely on the principle of God's great love and His liberality toward us. If God gave us His dearest gift, how will He withhold anything that benefits us and works to His glory?

He Wants My Life

In Matthew 16:24–28 we run into more thinking that seems backwards and upside down. What the Lord says is not what some people are expecting to hear. It seems to go against the grain of what they usually have been taught. It is hard to adjust to such a radical new way of looking at everything.

For instance, Jesus in this case appeals to the followers to identify with the cross. And the cross was a symbol of death. It is as though He were to say to us that a man should pick out his casket and then come follow Him.

What sort of appeal is that? How many people will respond to such a negative approach to recruiting?

Then Jesus follows up by saying that whoever will try to preserve his life will lose it, and whoever will lose his life, for the sake of Christ and the gospel, will really discover life.

These ground rules haven't changed. They are the same today. Any man who grasps at life and says to himself: "This is it, I'm going to live it up while I can," will come to the end of his trail and find that it hasn't been worth it. He gave himself to the things that are behind him, and life is spent. He is lost.

But the person who turns to God and says: "Lord, I want to give you everything I am, even life itself," will soon find that the dimensions of living change. Instead of the temporary values which he can pile up in the course of the seventy years or so that he has here, he is aiming at the sort of treasure that goes beyond his limited life span here. He is living for the real thing. He is laying up for himself treasure in heaven, where moths and rust and the corrupting things of this world cannot reach.

Jesus promises a day in which He will return with the Father, and with the angels who have been witnesses to what goes on here, and He will reward every man according to what he has done.

So it matters what you do. It matters what you do with the time that you have available today. It will either add up to something or to nothing. Which will it be in the long run?

It's like devaluation. When a nation changes its currency it scales down or eliminates the old and brings in the new. Then it matters a lot which currency you have in your pocket.

What currency are you dealing in?

He Wants My Good Works

"The proof of the pudding . . ."

Well, you know how it goes. You taste it and you soon know whether it's the real thing or not. What is true of the pudding is even more true of the Christian life.

It is quite impossible, according to James 2:14–26, to have a life based on faith in Jesus Christ without having a life that reflects the kind of love-in-action that characterized the Lord Jesus.

Yet anyone who looks around for the Christian community as it exists in the world today might be hard pressed to pick out the Christians from the rest of our society. They are not that distinctive, and it strongly suggests that something is seriously wrong.

All sorts of people carry the name Christian without carrying the imprint of Jesus Christ in their lives. And, if we understand James correctly, it doesn't add up.

Verbal declarations about faith are fine. James is not knocking that. But he states flatly that such affirmations of faith must be backed up by action if there is to be any proof of their reality.

How much Christian love is really put into action today? Certainly not as much as there should be. And often it is those who make the loudest statements about faith who are shortest on actions to back up the fact.

There is a beautiful harmony when faith and loving action (works) are found together. That is when faith comes shining through like light reflected from a brilliant diamond. You can tell it's the real thing.

And the two need to be together. There is an equal problem when anyone relies on works to fill in for a lack of faith. In this case it leads in the direction of foolish assumptions about works being the means through which we justify ourselves in the sight of God. That can never be. Paul spent a lot of time making that clear.

So, taken without each other, there are great problems. It's like a bicycle. You need both a back wheel and a front wheel to make it work—and some framing in between to hold them together, as well. When the whole system is tied together it can work beautifully. So it is with faith and works. They belong together.

This might be a good time to take inventory—to take stock in the churches we attend, and to ask ourselves about the small groups in which we are involved. Is there a good balance between faith and works? Or does it seem to you that most of the weight is placed on one or the other?

He Wants My Concern

The pot and the kettle are forever at each other —always calling each other black, but never seeing itself. The whole thing is figurative, of course, because in reality pots and kettles are not that sensitive to each other. But people are.

There is something about human nature, in its fallen condition, that rejoices in finding fault in others. This is a part of the self-justification instinct that seems to be a built-in factor of man's unregenerate nature. We try to scramble our way to righteousness over the bodies of others around us.

This phenomenon is so common that it can be observed every day of the week, to any one who is sensitive at all. Children have it as a favorite pastime. Johnny did it first. Or, Cindy isn't fair; she cheats; she doesn't like me.

So it goes, around and around. And when children grow up, they don't get over it. They just develop more subtle ways of expressing the same sort of thing.

It happens among groups too. Prejudices build up. One person thinks that all Negroes are . . . or all Jews try to . . . or those trashy, poor people who don't even . . . or . . . you name it. The instances of this kind of prejudice—unfair judgment—are so numerous we often miss them as they fly by in the course of a day's activities.

But we should catch them. And we should recognize them for what they are. And we should refuse to let them be any part of our thinking or our approach to life.

There is only one basis on which we can be justified before God. That is through the blood of our Saviour. It does no good to point out the faults of others, for we are never any more righteous because our sins are any less than the sins of others. We only hurt ourselves when we point to the sins, faults and imperfections of others around us. We are in no position to judge.

We have no room to boast, no matter how much it seems to us that we could do so because of our merits.

There is only room to rejoice in God's grace— and there is all the room in the world for that, and room in heaven too. So that is where our attention should be fixed.

When we develop that outlook, we will not be presumptuous. Everything rests on the providence of God. We move on from day to day realizing that our whole life rests in His hands. Read what James says in chapter 4:11–17.

He Wants My Action

Some people are noted for getting things done, while others just drift where the current takes them. Would you like to be the sort of person who accomplishes things to the glory of God?

The first step is to ask the Lord what needs doing—what He wants you involved in, of all the things you can think of. Make it specific, a task that can be started and then completed at some later date. And it should be something that can be evaluated—so that you can tell how well you did.

Then, with much prayer, throw yourself into the project. If it makes sense to do so, get others involved. Help get the job done through them. And help them feel the sense of accomplishment—even if you have to give up part of the credit in this process.

After you complete this project: Evaluate. Note where you could have done better. Then select another project and get started all over again.

CHAPTER 10

DO I REALLY NEED PEOPLE?

The New Testament portrait of the church of the first century is a striking contrast to anything that represents a general description of the church today. Anyone who takes time to read the book of Acts will be impressed with this fact. Few people would argue otherwise.

Why was the first century church so strong? Where did it get its vitality?

Many answers have been suggested, but two

points move into the foreground as primary reasons: (1) the early believers centered their existence in Jesus Christ and His resurrection, and (2) they built such a solid fellowship among themselves that their witness was practically indestructible.

We could use that outlook today.

Even Outsiders?

Peter wasn't one to fool around with a lot of diplomatic niceties. Right to the point. No matter which way it cut. That was Peter—after the Pentecostal infilling of the Spirit, as well as before it.

In Acts 2:41–47 Peter had just delivered his powerful message at Pentecost, when the church had come alive in the power of the Holy Spirit as Jesus had promised. Some 3,000 people had responded affirmatively to Peter's message. The decision was clear—whether to accept Jesus as the Messiah or to side with those who had unjustly crucified Him. These 3,000 new believers added greatly to the strength of that early church.

It must have been a traumatic experience for those who had actually been with Jesus and in close fellowship with each other. Now they had to throw open their circle of fellowship to receive a vast number of newcomers, which must have included many strangers from other places in the Mediterranean world.

Some pass off this great influx of new believers as a simple description of what happened at that particular moment in the life of the church. They reject the idea that it should be normative—the way the church should be, at other times in its history. Yet we are drawn back to Jesus' statement as to what would and what should happen in the experience of the church.

Just before He ascended into heaven, Jesus said: "But ye shall receive power, after that the Holy Ghost is come upon you: and ye shall be witnesses unto me" (Acts 1:8). This incident in receiving 3,000 members into the believing community was one indicator of the power of the Spirit at work in the church.

But notice that this power of the Spirit both began in fellowship and resulted in it. At the very beginning of Acts 2 it says that the followers of Jesus were "all with one accord in one place." And at the end of this same chapter it says that they "continued steadfastly in the apostles' doctrine and fellowship, and in breaking of bread, and in prayers."

Fellowship *is* the norm. Without it the church has never been strong. The best way to understand revival and evangelism is to think of it in terms of intensified fellowship—like warm embers which are brought into contact with each other and produce a flaming heat.

Other Christians?

Some people react negatively to the word "fellowship." To them the word suggests something very saccharine, even sticky. And perhaps impractical. They picture it as a rosy glow over everything—a sort of super-spiritual bowing and scraping that is supposed to make other people feel good all the time. To them it seems that this is badly out of line with life. And they are right! If that is what the term fellowship means, we should have ditched it long ago. If the Christian life boils down to some rosy glow of pretense which we pull over the realities of our existence, we are in bad trouble.

Fellowship—as we use the term anyway—is something very different. It is rooted in a common recognition, a common loyalty, a common allegiance, to Jesus Christ. He is the one who makes it possible. It all centers in the recognition of Him as the one Mediator between God and man.

Once you see that, the rest should become clear. Our relationships to each other should be clear. Our roles in serving, helping, witnessing, ministering and administering should become clear. Everything begins to fit together as we see Jesus Christ at the center of the believing community. It is in Him that we find all our basic needs.

Interestingly, the very things that many critics of the church want to see in the world are things that should be encompassed in Christian fellowship. Many radicals have recently scorched the church for "not really caring" about people.

What a reproof! In the first century, the very opposite was true. Christians were the minority community that really did care about people. They cared about each other. And they cared about everyone else too.

In Galatians 6 Paul shows how very practical

Christian fellowship really is. He expects something of these people—attitudes and actions that will result in the healthy growth of the whole believing community.

If the Christian community is to make an impact on today's world, it will have to take a lesson from these Christians of the first century.

What's Wrong with Me?

The odds against the early Christian movement surviving were millions to one.

Yet in another sense it couldn't fail. Its strength lay in its unwavering faith in the risen Christ. In fact these Christians identified so fully with Jesus Christ that they felt they shared in the resurrection experience. They were new people.

When Peter and John were on trial, their wisdom and their sense of God's presence within them was so noticeable that the authorities were reminded of Jesus Himself. See Acts 4:13.

New men.

New in Christ.

That's reality. That's power. That's living.

And that's what *we* need.

As soon as that gets straightened out, everything else should begin to shape up. And to make sure nobody misunderstands what should exemplify the Christian life, Paul gives some specifics in Colossians 3:1–11.

The new man soon understands that the things that really count are the things that go beyond our temporary existence here. This is the currency that involves Christ, other people and eternity. It is expansive. Every day is a new adventure with God when you enter life at this point.

This kind of living has no place for petty prejudices, self-indulgence, jealousy, sexual promiscuity, anger, maliciousness or similar ends which are so often the underlying (although cleverly hidden) motivations in much of life around us today.

Discrimination is out. Acceptance of everyone, just as you find him, is the policy. It is God's policy, and how can ours be less? God is not in the business of turning people away. Anyone who follows His program will find openings to people in all directions. There are simply no limitations.

Christians are really a new race of men!

They are to square with each other.

They are to live for each other's benefit.

Their personality traits are to be: integrity, honesty, unselfishness, unpushiness, consideration, joy, peace, and outgoing concern.

But the skeptic says: "Yeah, show me!"

And we had better be ready to show him.

What's-His-Name

The practicalities of Christian fellowship are often lost amid the formalities of today's religion. It is perfectly possible to go to a church service in almost any city, participate fully in the worship program, and yet come away feeling totally anonymous.

This is not entirely the fault of the church. To

some extent it is due to the changes which have taken place in our modern social structures.

The city itself is a place of massive anonymity. It is simply impossible for people to be involved in any deep, meaningful sense with more than a few score or perhaps a few hundred people. Certain personalities influence many more people than that, but they are not involved in continuing two-way interactions with them.

When it comes to deep, meaningful interaction with people on a continuing basis, the number is cut back to the few. Yet there is great strength in the relationship to the few—if that relationship runs according to the biblical norm.

In accepting Christ, we open ourselves to accepting each other. We may not like all of the personality traits in another Christian to whom we are close, and we may see plenty of room for improvement, but we can do nothing but accept him as a brother. And we may see Christ using us to lead him toward constructive changes. We realize, of course, that we too are very imperfect, and there may be many other points in which our own lives should be improving in order to live up to the potential that Christ wants to live out through us. Another Christian alongside of us may be the one to help us on those points.

This element of mutual help and improvement is very much lacking in the church today. It is curious that self-improvement programs today are almost entirely under the auspices of "secular" organizations, especially the educational institutions. Yet the fact is, there are some areas of personal improvement that can hardly be handled by any other institution than the church—in its true role as the believing community.

Paul points the way to this kind of growth as a function of "the word of Christ" which dwells within us richly. Then we come into the sort of fellowship where our lives are constantly upbuilding each other. See Colossians 3:12–17.

Two Dimensions

If fellowship in the vertical dimension is diminished or cut off, fellowship in the horizontal dimension is likely to be all out of alignment. It's like a car that doesn't know where its hind wheels are; it tries to go in two different directions at once.

Spiritually, our lives are realigned through fellowship upward—"truly our fellowship is with the Father, and with his Son Jesus Christ" (I John 1:3). That was why John was writing—to give witness to what God had done in Christ. He came as the one source of light through which men could find God.

As men find God, they find each other. There is much in today's world that seems to go against that logic. It seems that all sorts of well-intentioned causes, which may be anything but Christian, may be reaching out to help people in their need. Many times they are more effective than the Christian body. Then how can we say that men first find God, and then find each other?

There are many cases when men happen upon parts of God's truth and apply it. They have a part of the truth but not the essential center. Their actions may be good, and entirely commendable. Their problem lies in the fact that they have not seen the fullness of the truth in Jesus Christ.

Then too, there are many instances where the truth of Christ has gotten through to people in the past, and certain of their Christian insights live on in the actions of those who have followed them. This is sort of a cultural afterglow which can be observed in so-called Christian cultures. But the afterglow always fades.

Again, the only corrective is to get back to the fullness of the light in Jesus Christ. Back to the truth which John was declaring.

Once the light of Jesus Christ enters the situation it banishes darkness and it brings newness of life. No more walking in spiritual and moral darkness.

Christians are bearers of light. And the source of that light is the source of their fellowship. As they are together in Christ they illuminate each other and they lighten the world around them.

Love Is for People

Throughout the centuries, men have sought to glorify God in many ways.

They have built great cathedrals, rendered magnificent paintings, written and performed beautiful music. Others have dedicated their lives to serving God and man in other ways. Some have gained world attention, some have served unnoticed.

But the one thing that pleases God most is available to everyone—especially to the one who knows Jesus Christ.

Love.

It pleases Him.

It glorifies God!

If you want to accomplish something great, explore John's advice in I John 4. "Love is of God." Love is the language in which we can be sure to please God, for it is His language. He used it first, and proved to the world His love through the sacrifice of His own Son for our salvation.

Learn that language. It communicates when everything else seems useless. It will remake your life. It will draw you out of yourself and your inner problems, and it will focus your attention on others around you.

Nobody has ever seen God, as John points out in verse 12. But they do see God at work when they see love—the love demonstrated by the life of the Christian who is open to God.

Start with those of your own family, and others very close to you. Ask yourself what you can do to demonstrate your love for them. Then set about doing it, right away, before other routine activities crowd in, to crowd out love.

That is probably why Satan is called the god of this world. He has managed to set up such a system here that we get involved with it very easily—Now, let's see . . . I've got to pay these bills . . . and make that appointment . . . and get to that meeting . . . and . . . and . . . and. . . .

It never ends. There is always more to do than

can be done. So it is all the more important to do those things which need doing most.

And before everything else comes love.

If love means so much to God, how can we settle for anything less?

Equal Before God

The gospel is a universal message. It is directed to everyone. Nobody is left out. God's love in Christ is all-encompassing.

It was important for the early Christians to realize this, for the Christian message had sprung out of a Jewish background. It could have been left at that, as some kind of addition to Jewish religion. But that was not God's plan.

God was out to reach the whole world in Jesus Christ. There was one great human problem—sin. And in Jesus Christ, God paid the price of man's sin. Now it was time to let the world know, and to bring about the reconciliation between God and man which Christ had made possible.

The Christians at Ephesus were mainly Gentiles, not Jews by birth. Thus Paul had pointed out that they were alien to Israel and not included in the covenant promises which God had made available to Israel. They were without God and without hope in the world, Paul said. Read Ephesians 2:11–22.

But then came Jesus Christ, and in His blood (verse 13) Jews and Gentiles were brought together. Any estrangement that had existed previously, no longer belonged. God had broken down the whole logic of their separation.

In Jesus Christ, and in light of the good news of what He accomplished for mankind, all men stand equal before God. They may not be equal in talents, or gifts, or many other aspects of their lives. But they are equal in one all-important respect. They have equal access to God's grace through the blood of Jesus Christ.

This makes all the difference. All men meet at the cross.

In light of this, it is impossible to consider "Christian" anything that separates men, or makes second-class citizens of some. If all men stand equal at the cross, how can we treat them as anything less than that in other relations? Prejudice and discrimination are not from Jesus Christ. He is the Way to God for *all* men.

Thus Paul says that Gentiles are "fellow-citizens" with the saints—those people whom God had previously set apart as His people.

To *everyone* who believes in Christ comes the promise of acceptance in the household of God.

Who's My Brother?

The kind of fellowship we have been considering is one of the greatest needs in existence today. Only as the body is strengthened and renewed in fellowship will it be able to reach out and influence the world. Every Christian can do his part to strengthen the fellowship, if he will just take the time.

Decide that you are going to bring people together in Christian fellowship. If you are already in one small group that meets for fellowship and prayer, ask whether you should be starting another one. Ask yourself whom you might contact. Which of your contacts might benefit most from meeting together? Some might be very strong Christians. Others might not even know the Lord yet. But you will see great things happen as you bring them together to share their mutual concerns, and to pray.

CHAPTER 11

MUST I LOVE ALL CHRISTIANS?

What is the test of truth?

This is a question that has been discussed a great deal down through the centuries. In answer to it credal statements have been formulated, books written, doctrinal positions stated, dogmas promulgated, ecclesiastical laws decreed, conciliar statements issued, sermons preached, appeals made, and demonstrations staged. While each of these may have had its effect, has any of them finally and for all time proved the truth?

God's Word is truth, and it centers in the person of His Son, Jesus Christ.

But how is the world to know? What is the

proof? In terms of everyday activity the proof that God has intended is the love and concern which should be seen in the life of the believer.

This should be testimony to the truth just as the life of Jesus was itself a witness to His own identity.

Love is not ornamentation for the Christian life —it *is* the Christian life.

Where Do I Walk?

The Christian life is no pushover.

Many people may think it is. After all, it's just a matter of making sure you don't do anyone any harm, applying the golden rule, and generally doing the right thing. People who think that way usually pride themselves on being upright, and pretty well suited to the kingdom of heaven. They may even be humble enough not to say it that way. But they think it.

And how wrong they are!

Anyone who thinks that way is dead wrong— both dead and wrong. For there is nothing whatever Christian about that mode of thinking. It is completely self-centered. It is based entirely on one's pride in one's own actions, which is always wrong.

God is the assessor of our attitudes and actions. We are the custodians of them.

But how are we to assure that our attitudes and actions will be those that glorify God, and bring men to recognize Him?

Paul's answer to this is in Galatians 5: "Walk in

the Spirit." Then he points out that the Spirit and the flesh are constantly at war with each other. They contradict each other. Consequently there is a certain tension which the Christian experiences—the tension of the man's natural desires being at odds with the leading of the Spirit.

Paul says that the secret is giving place to the Spirit, and when any Christian does that the Spirit displaces the sinful desires which spring up so naturally within.

But let's have this in everyday terms. How does the Christian "walk in the Spirit"? Does he just try to perform the good deeds mentioned in this section, as contrasted to the bad, and then figure that he is in the Spirit to the extent that he succeeds?

No. It won't work. You know from experience it won't work. So how do you walk in the Spirit?

It is really a matter of faith—seeing things as they really are. It is one thing to verbalize about our belief. It is another thing to believe.

When we really see God, and Christ, and the Holy Spirit, and the world, and sin, and our own sinful selves in perspective, it drives us to God. What can we do but cry out for His mercy? Then we see our lack of love. We see God's desire to love others through us. That is the result of faith. That is perspective. And that is basic to walking in the Spirit.

Basic Training

Christian concern is based on God's action in about the same way that flight is based on the laws of aerodynamics. Without an understanding of the foundational principles, nothing else makes much sense.

The average person, living apart from any relationship to God, has little chance of getting airborne. He hasn't discovered the basics. He might do a lot of things that somehow look like the motions of flight. But he doesn't really fly.

He can persuade himself that he is proceeding in the right direction ethically. He can exert enough effort to get going at quite a speed, other things considered. He can convince himself he is really doing all right. But he still isn't flying.

To fly is something else. It must take place on the basis of the laws that govern flight.

Likewise love.

There are times when the world seems better at expressing love than the Christian community. That is sad. God expects quite another order of response from those who are His.

Christians should be the ones to out-love all the rest of the world put together!

It is in the very nature of things.

For the Christian, this is the way to fly.

It all begins in the fact that God has redeemed us. See I Peter 1:18,19. He did this through a currency that goes far beyond all the wealth in the world. Nothing compares with it. God could more easily have spent twenty million stars and a thousand universes than He could the lifeblood of His Son.

Yet God paid the price.

That is how much He loved us.

And what follows?

"See that ye love one another with a pure heart fervently" (verse 22). This Christian concern is as basic as anything can be. Without the constant expression of love, especially for others who follow Jesus Christ, nothing about the Christian walk comes off real.

The only way to get away from the phony—the earthbound performance of good works in a purely mechanical way—is to get back to what God has done for us in Christ.

Then everything comes alive. And love is real.

I Can't Do It Alone!

The sign of eternal life is love.

Whoever doesn't exhibit love for other believers has the mark of death on him.

John puts it just that flatly in I John 3.

In fact, he adds that anyone who doesn't care about a fellow-Christian is tantamount to a murderer. And murderers don't possess eternal life.

In other words, unloving Christians aren't Christians. That is what his statement amounts to.

Then John gets embarrassingly practical. He mentions specifics—like sharing possessions. If a brother has plenty and sees another Christian living in poverty, he should be right there to share the wealth.

But that's not patriotic!

Never mind. It's Christian.

When will we learn to believe God? When will we take Him seriously?

We spend so much time wrapped up in our concerns about this life. Business calls us o'er the tumult of this life's wild restless sea. We can't even hear Jesus.

Or perhaps it's pleasure, or education, or family, or sports, or a million other things. But not God's concerns for men.

God *is* concerned. He sees the sparrow fall. And He numbers the hairs of our head. He loves every last man, woman and child in this world. He gave His life to set up a relationship with His creatures. Yet men go on spurning His love. Still He goes on loving them.

But how do they know?

They should know it through us—through every last believer. Christians should be so genuinely concerned for each other that they really expend themselves in service, with great joy.

In one sense it is a duty. But in another sense it is not a duty at all. Anyone who has really been in love knows what this means. Nothing is a duty when love is in the picture. Everything is done in a thrilling sense of relationship.

That is the way we are intended to pour ourselves out in love. Nothing could make more sense.

To the Christian who is really in touch with Christ nothing comes more naturally than love.

And nothing could be more genuine, for then it becomes God's love expressed through us.

But God Loves Them!

Each of us lives on the brink of eternity.

It is only a breath away.

Then the judgment, as we stand before Jesus Christ to report on the deeds done in the body—the things accomplished on earth.

We have such a little bit of time in which to serve! It's so short!

Yet God promises that our short lives can be significant, and in ways available to every one of us. Love is a commodity anyone can develop. The more it is expressed, the more one has left.

But the fact that our time is short demands that we use it well. Peter makes this clear. Then he follows up with a suggestion. Here's the best investment that can possibly be made of time in the service of Christ: "Above all things have fervent charity among yourselves" (I Peter 4:8).

Is that all?

That's it. Love sums it all up. Jesus said that. Love God, and then your neighbor—that is the summary of the whole law. Once we catch onto that fact, it sets a lot of other things straight. Like pretensions of piousness. That goes right out the window when we start practicing love as Christ meant it.

Then everyone begins to find his place. As God has distributed His gifts to the church, each member finds his role, and he accepts it, meanwhile also receiving benefit from the ministries of others in the body. So the system gets functioning in good order.

One member preaches, while another serves in other ways.

But the net result is the glory of God. God is

pleased with the church when it functions as He intended it to. He looks upon it as His bride. He delights in her. He loves her. Nothing could please Him better than to have her in good health, and loving in Him, as He loves her.

Too ideal? Unrealistic?

Well, perhaps it doesn't seem to be the way the church usually functions or relates to its Lord. Human frailties and sinful intrusions seem all too evident.

Perhaps we should just accept the ideal, and not be thrown by the inconsistencies of the present church. So, as best we can we help the church fit that ideal, and leave the rest to Christ.

Out of Focus

Some people can't stand poverty.

Others can't stand riches.

Paul learned to live with both. At times he had more than enough. At other times he had nothing. But it didn't matter. These were trivial considerations. See Philippians 4:10—20.

But they are not trivial to most of us today.

No indeed.

We spend most of our time with these "trivialities." How much of our time is spent on the house —getting it, paying for it, maintaining it, decorating it, improving it, landscaping it, and then selling it for a better location?

And how much of our time is spent on food— shopping, cooking, baking, serving, barbequing and then doing the dishes?

And how much time do we spend on clothes, sports, recreation, and so many other such activities?

It would be senseless to suggest that these could be completely ruled out of our lives. But we should raise the question whether these things serve us. Or do we serve them? Is there some sense in which they all fit into some overall dimension of service to Jesus Christ?

When that happens we find that housing, and meals, and clothes and all the other items of life around us begin to fit into a pattern that adds up to the glory of God.

Then too, there is a relatedness to the rest of the Christian family. Friendliness, hospitality, entertaining (both brothers and strangers) comes naturally when we open our homes to the service of Christ. We find people whose lives we touch daily being served through our contacts, our concern and our caring actions. God must fit the whole program together, and He must be free to do it from day to day.

Then the daily activities of life become sacraments. Christ lives in us, and God can be glorified even in the smallest things we do.

Relatedness to other people, especially to those who share the love of God in Christ, is the key to this sort of living.

We are outlets for His love, and He supplies everything we need in accord with His riches in glory by Christ Jesus.

This is the perspective of true concern.

Sounding Brass and Tinkling Cymbals

God contradicts Himself.

That is what the people must have thought as they heard Isaiah's prophecy (1:12—17). Wasn't it God who had given the command for these sacrifices—the oblations, the incense, the observance of the new moons and the sabbaths, the assemblies, the solemn meetings, the feasts? All of these are written into the law. It is written right there in Leviticus, and in Numbers and in the other books of the law.

And when they did what God ordered, He declared that He was dissatisfied. He was weary of their performance, and told them to stop. How inconsistent! How temperamental! What did God want anyway?

Those people didn't see themselves, any more than we see ourselves today. For we have the same problem. We are just like those people, and God speaks to us through Isaiah as much as He spoke to them.

Vain performances.

Much activity in the name of the church and Christian organizations comes right into that category. We think we are pleasing God and we are just making Him sick and tired, and weary.

When will we wake up?

The problem in Isaiah's time was that the performance was not based on a heart attitude that was open to God. Imagine what would happen at a symphony concert if every musician sat down and simply played the notes on the paper—without responding to the conductor or keeping in harmony and in time with each other!

That is just what was happening in Judah.

And that is what is happening in much of Christendom today. We beat out the required notes but the harmony, the real music, is missing. It's nothing more than noise.

So what does God really want?

He wants us to turn our hearts back to Him, put nonsense aside, and "Learn to do well; seek judgment, relieve the oppressed, judge the fatherless, plead for the widow" (verse 17).

That is godly concern.

It is rooted in God's love for all men, and it is directly related to what He did for us in Jesus Christ.

Do I Want to Love Them?

Whose opinions are you most concerned about?

Your own, or those of other Christians?

Do you live to please yourself? Or others? Or God? In what order?

Occasionally you meet Christians who have really sold out to God. Somehow you can tell. They may not be perfect, but they are living a distinctive type of life—one that is lived mostly outside themselves.

In some ways they move through life just like other people, yet they are very unlike other people. Perhaps you can see it in the fact that some things don't seem to conern them so much. Their priorities are set on the values that count over the long haul. They are not thrown off by the mundane items of their day-to-day experience. Yet everything seems to get sorted into position after all. And you wonder how.

There is a principle in this kind of existence. "Seek ye first the kingdom of God, and his righteousness;" Jesus said, "and all these things shall be added unto you" (Matthew 6:33). And that is just the way it works. There are some Christians who have found that to be true, because they have tried it. They have put it into practice. It meets the test of real-life application.

God is invisible, and that throws many people. They need something visible to go by. But God has chosen not to be seen, except in His Son who lived and died for us.

But God does move around in this world. He moves through it and acts within it. Yet many people fail to see Him. The fact is, God is usually working through other people. He chooses human instruments to do what He wants to do in the world.

Thus, to find God at work in the world, watch people. Some people are being used by God in wonderful ways—although they may not be attended by any sort of publicity. Other people, although professing Christians, are hardly available to God. And some are not available to God at all, but they may be going through a softening up process which God sometimes allows.

The chief clue is the degree in which Christians are concerned about other people around them. This is the major means through which God chooses to work. Anyone who is open to this sort of concern is open to the working of God in his life.

Outgoing concern is the key.

It is impossible to live the Christian life in isolation. God never wanted isolation Himself and didn't intend it for His people.

To be Christian means to be a part of a community of faith and a community of love. Concern for each other is intended to be the normal Christian experience today.

Determine to help change that. The church must return to the standard of loving concern which its Lord set for it. You can be a part of the restoration. Decide to help, and begin today.

CHAPTER 12

HOW HIGH IS UP?

Which way is up?

That is the feeling you get when you read certains parts of the Bible. In the Gospels, you sense it whenever Jesus is speaking. Then in Paul's letters, you come across it again. The Acts of the Apostles reflects it in action, and Peter and the other New Testament writers have it too.

It's that upside down (or rather rightside up!) sense of values. So often you see these early Christians looking at things from such a different perspective than the world around them.

And so they should. That is what conversion to Jesus Christ means. Their lives and their writings were consistent with what they believed.

But what of Christians today? Do you find it difficult to think of Christians who really think this same way today?

And about the only way to correct that is to saturate ourselves in the thinking and writing of those men who learned it from Jesus Himself.

Face Up!

Scholars have sometimes charged that Paul was a madman. He was psychotic, they say. He had an obsession. It drove him to insane ends.

Given certain assumptions, there is a certain sense in which they are right. See Philippians 3:12–21.

Often the test of normality is the ability to adjust to the values and thought patterns of the world around you—to fit in. And, it must be admitted that Paul, along with most of the other early Christians, didn't do that at all well. They just were not the type to fit into the value system of their world.

Not that they were cantankerous or hostile. Not at all. They were the most peaceable people that anyone could ask for. Yet, oddly, there was trouble wherever they went.

They had a reputation.

"These that have turned the world upside down are come hither also" (Acts 17:6).

Here were these peace-loving, gentle people who never sought to do anyone any harm turning the world upside down. What was it about them that gave them that reputation? There must have been some reason for it.

The reason was deep in their own character. They had sold out to Jesus the Nazarene. He was their Lord. Their entire view of life revolved around Him. What He had said when bodily present among them formed the basis for their outlook on life. And one great fact kept always coming to the foreground of their thinking. They even greeted each other with it.

He is risen!

He is risen indeed!

Nothing else counted. Paul makes this clear. He had counted everything as loss, in order that he might know Jesus Christ (Philippians 3:7–11). His former reputation for strictly keeping the Jewish law meant nothing. Even life itself meant nothing. He was like a man already dead.

He *was* already dead—to all the former values of his life.

But it wasn't his thought to look back on past experiences. No, he was looking ahead. And pressing ahead. For ahead he saw the person of Jesus Christ and the prize of the Master.

Life was like a race to him. And he was ready always to give it everything he had—to run the race and gain the prize. And he leaves us with this thought—

Press on.

Add Up!

In the process of greeting the Christians to whom he was writing, Peter mentions the name of Jesus Christ, the Lord. (See II Peter 1:3–11.) And thereupon he bursts into ecstatic praise at the marvels of God's grace.

It is just like Peter.

Ecstatic!

But genuine, just the same.

Peter had good reason to be ecstatic, for he knew by personal experience how Jesus Christ, through the presence of His indwelling Holy Spirit, could empower the life of the Christian.

"Partakers of the divine nature," is what he calls it.

Do you know what that means?

It means just what it says. There is no other way to understand Peter, and no other way to understand the rest of the New Testament. God wants us to partake of His nature. That is what the ministry of the Holy Spirit is all about.

Some people may interpret that in terms of a mystical experience—a trip away off on some very spiritual cloud.

But not Peter.

From his ecstatic recognition of what it means to have this relationship with God, Peter suddenly gets very practical.

Add to your faith virtue.

Virtue is a very practical, observable, tangible human quality. No mystical guesswork where virtue is concerned. The Christian knows when he is virtuous. And so does the world.

Add to your virtue knowledge.

Knowledge, too, is tangible and practical. It involves thoughtful discernment, good judgment, and an understanding of God's will.

Add temperance.
Add patience.
Add godliness.
Add brotherly kindness.
Add love.

How practical can you get? This is God's recipe for fruitfulness.

If you have these ingredients, you should be fruitful and have a clear road ahead in performing the will of God.

If you don't have them, Christian, you are blind.

"Up, Up and Away"

Every butterfly has gone through the stage when it could only crawl, it could not fly. It was, in its former state, an earthbound caterpillar. One wonders if it had even dreamed of flying in its lowly condition.

But then came conversion.

Changes began to take place in the larva, and it spun a cocoon. There it passed into a new stage of life. And when it emerged it was no longer an earthbound caterpillar, but rather an adult butterfly.

The difference between the caterpillar and the butterfly is striking. But no more striking than the difference between the man who is earthbound, or outside of Christ, and the man who is in the Spirit.

Theirs are two distinct ways of life.

One crawls, the other flies.

To those who observe from other worlds, the one

is ugly and despicable, while the other is charming and delightful.

The natural man, in his condition apart from God, can only crawl. He is limited to the movements of crawling—without fellowship with God he cannot pray, or worship, or witness, or draw on the strength of God's grace in Jesus Christ. He is not fitted for any of these things.

But God has better things for the man who responds to His urgings. He converts. In recognizing and accepting Jesus Christ he enters the conversion stage of his existence. He becomes a new man. Read Romans 8:1–11.

And when he emerges he has a new way of life.

It is a sad fact, however, that the analogy breaks down. In the spiritual sense, many butterflies spend most of their lives crawling. They rarely test their wings. They have not thrown off the former self completely.

Thus Paul urges in Ephesians 4:22 that Christians throw off the old man.

Christians who are motivated just like anyone else along the street haven't begun to live. They are not using their wings. They are earthbound when they should be flying.

This is the law of the Spirit of life in Christ Jesus. God is eager that His righteousness might be fulfilled in us, who walk not after the flesh but after the Spirit. We can never please God as long as we are earthbound.

We must live up to our potential in the Spirit.

There is no other way to fly!

Look Up!

Put on the new man, Paul says in Ephesians 4:24.

Let the Spirit of God dwell in you, he says in Romans 8:12–17.

These are two ways of saying the same thing. God is invading this world in a quiet but wonderful way. He is invading it through an army of new men and women—those who have turned to Jesus Christ and allowed the Holy Spirit to dwell in them.

New life is theirs. The energy of the Spirit becomes a moving force in any life that is given to Him. Things begin to happen. God goes to work. His mode of work may not always be dramatic by the world's standards. But that is not the point. Who cares for the world's standards as a measurement of what God is doing? We need to be satisfied just in the fact that our lives are really available to God, and if that is true we can be sure God will be at work.

Anyone who is committed to Jesus Christ is not bound to live according to the motivations of his fallen nature. He has a new nature. He has been freed to respond to the Spirit. But it is still a matter of his choosing.

God has not chosen to work through robots. He wants to work through willing, responsive beings. That has been His plan from the beginning, and He will not go against it. God only works where there is a willingness to have Him work.

Discovering this fact is a big part of the Christian life. It is not just a matter of having a new set of rules to live by—that would be pretty mechanical too.

God needs more flexibility than that. He needs the open heart, the open life through which to reach out and touch others and bring them to Himself as well. Thus the attitude of openness to God, to His Son and to His Holy Spirit spreads, and God is pleased. For it is through these means that God is extending Himself into this world.

Most of us would prefer a dramatic crusade of conquest. There is something about that sort of operation that attracts us. Now God is more often pleased to work in quiet, almost imperceptible ways. And if that is the way He wants to work what have we to say against it?

The important thing is to put on the new man and be available to the Spirit.

Stir Up!

God makes His gifts available to the members of the community of believers so that they might be used. He must be displeased, therefore, when they fall into disuse. Paul did not want this to happen to Timothy, his much loved son in the Lord.

In opening his second letter to Timothy Paul has indicated his thankfulness and his personal affection for him (1:3—7). He longs to see him, and thinks back to previous times that they had together. And he remembers the faith which Timothy had, and the great faith of his mother and grandmother.

Then, as if a slight cloud of concern crossed his mind, Paul exhorted Timothy to "stir up" the gift of God that was in him.

What caused Paul to say this?

There is no indication in this letter, or anywhere else, that Timothy had turned away from the faith. But there is indication that his fervor in the things of the Lord had cooled a little, perhaps because he had been so long away from the fellowship with Paul. This would explain the warmth of Paul's opening remarks. While they were fully sincere they may also have been a personal way of reminding Timothy of the warmth of the fellowship previously experienced.

Underlying this reminder which Paul sends off to Timothy we can see one of the primary principles of Christian life and experience in these earliest years of the Christian era. That principle was fellowship. These Christians made it a point to be together, to support each other, to pray together, and to reinforce each others' walk with the Lord.

Now that he was removed from the fellowship to which he was accustomed, Timothy might have slipped a little in the intensity of his love for Christ. This might also be indicated in chapter 2:4 where Paul points out that a good soldier should never be entangled "with the affairs of this life."

Back in chapter 1:7, we may have another clue to the problem. Perhaps Timothy's former fearlessness, his power in the Holy Spirit, had given way to a spirit of timidity or weakness.

In any case, Paul had a suggested solution. Rekindle the gift of God, he told him. Evidently Timothy had previously been given this gift through the laying on of hands. Now it was time to stir it up again.

Wise Up!

"Put them in mind . . ." Paul told Titus (Titus 3:1).

There are times when Christians need a word of instruction, and sometimes of rebuke and of correction.

Then sparks begin to fly. And that is the sign of immaturity in the Christian life.

Mature individuals can take proper criticism. They can weigh it for its worth and they can apply it where it needs to be applied. They grow by it.

But immature people cannot take criticism. Regardless of the truth or applicability of the criticism, they cannot accept it. They react. They get defensive. All sorts of new mechanisms come into play. They simply cannot accept the well-intentioned criticism for what it is worth. Consequently, they cannot benefit by it.

But that does not lessen the need for the Christian to be corrected. There are times when those who have gained mature judgment in the things of Christ must speak out. They will be remiss in their duty if they do not.

Speaking out is a Christian duty too.

Great discretion is needed in the way one speaks out, however. The relative maturity of the Christian to be corrected or rebuked must be kept in mind. The net effect of the impact of words needs to be calculated ahead of time.

This does not mean you would back away from facing the truth of the situation. That too would be very harmful—and it is probably what is done too often when reprimand is needed.

So be sure to speak out when that is what is needed, but do it carefully, always checking your own motives to make sure that your real purpose is to help.

If you arrive at this place where you are willing to speak out, as Paul indicated that Titus should, you will find this to be a real part of your ministry to other Christians. But great caution is needed in exercising this gift. Misused, it can do real harm.

So, speak out . . . carefully.

Head Up!

Finally, we come back to Paul's model of the Christian community—the body. See Ephesians 4:1–7.

This is the ideal of the total system at work. There are different members with different functions. Each is meant to be in its own place, performing its proper function. If it is not, there is trouble. Or, if a particular member is envious of the function of another member, there is trouble.

The body must respond to the center of the whole system—the head—in order to function properly. There is no life apart from a direct connection with the head. And the whole body must be nourished by the bloodstream.

There is just one body, Paul says.

This is something to remember, and perhaps

something to be disturbed by, in a day when there are so many factions, splinters, splits and substructures in the Christian community. Some have called it a scandal. And it is.

But the answer is not simple realignment of organizations. That is too artificial. It is like suggesting that carpentry is needed to put the body back together again.

The body is meant to be unified. But unity is the result of responding genuinely to the head, which is Jesus Christ.

The spirit which promotes unity is indicated in verse 3—"Endeavoring to keep the unity of the Spirit in the bond of peace." This rules out motivations of personal pride, self-aggrandizement and faction building. Instead, it leads to common concern, brotherly love, willingness for others to lead where God has given them ability, and rejoicing in watching the growth of others in Christ.

That is the working system. The healthy body is a working model of the Christian life.

There is a military counterpart to this model. We see a platoon of soldiers marching across the drill field, rank upon rank, in perfect step. Then they are brought to a halt, put at ease and allowed to dismiss. Rank and order seem to disintegrate. But after a few minutes another order is given.

Fall in!

Order returns. The platoon moves off as a unit, subject to one person's command. They perform as a single body.

It is time for Christians to fall in.

Shape Up!

Look back over the subjects which we have studied each day this week. Then take a piece of paper and list the subjects down the left side of the page, allowing space between them.

Now make a scale on which you can rate yourself, or your small group, with regard to each subject. (If you are unclear about the point of any of these subjects, go back and read the Scriptures again.) The results should look something like the following:

Face Up

1	2	3	4	5	6	7	8	9	10

Add Up

1	2	3	4	5	6	7	8	9	10

(and so on.)

Then rate yourself on each of the seven subjects. Ten represents an unbeatable score—perfection. And zero represents miserable failure.

It will also be helpful to make a similar chart and rate the small group in which you are involved. Admittedly, these evaluations must be very subjective, but they should lead to recognition of places where improvement can be achieved.

CHAPTER 13

WHEN DO I ARRIVE?

Criticism of the church is a popular sport these
days. Many people enter into it with great vigor.
They accuse it of being out of touch with the
world—"irrelevant" is the word for it. They point
out that many professing Christians are hypocrites.
Instead of being characterized by outgoing love,
they say that church members are more interested
in their own social status and self-justification.

The thing that gives a sting to this critique is the
fact that there is often considerable validity to it.

In some ways the critics may see the church more clearly than those on the inside—as far as the behavior of its members is concerned.

So, the church must see itself. It doesn't have to be popular, but it should be respected. It must let God mold its character. Then it needs to set in motion a program of training that will bring it to be what it should be—a usable tool in God's hands.

Really Know God

The buildup of human knowledge in recent decades has been so rapid that it is almost impossible to imagine. It is estimated that human knowledge doubled between the year A.D. 1 and 1750. It doubled again between 1750 and 1900. It doubled the third time between 1900 and 1950, and the fourth time between 1950 and 1960. Thus, in only ten years it doubled, whereas it once took 1750 years.

The recent buildup is partly due to new ways of handling information, and of cutting into it to get at the facts. Human experience and knowledge of hard facts can be searched and compared in new and wonderful ways.

And to a great extent this vast new body of information is rapidly changing our way of life and the life of many others in our world. A good example is the ability of man to venture into space and explore it. Through good management vast numbers of people and their skills can be related to each other in effective ways.

The landing of men on the moon in July 1969 for instance was estimated to involve some 400,000 people through a vast network of contracts and subcontracts which were let by the National Aeronautics and Space Administration.

The successful completion of that moon mission represented a new stage in the capabilities of man to use the buildup of knowledge in attaining goals which he selects.

But things must be kept in perspective. There are still many things man cannot do. When a cat is killed in the street, man is helpless to restore the cat to life.

There is also question about *how* man uses the vast amounts of knowledge that are available to him.

That gets us back to wisdom, which is something else again. Wisdom is based on true insights, which in turn rest upon valid assumptions about the real nature of the world. And that is where we meet God. See Proverbs 2:1–8.

To be truly wise then, a man must be in touch with God and the wisdom that is from God. This is just as true today as it was many hundreds of years before Christ when Solomon wrote his Proverbs. The real nature of the world has not changed, in spite of the great buildup in knowledge.

But to the man who has eyes that see, and ears that hear, the buildup in human knowledge can be another path that leads to the knowledge of God and effective service to Him.

Know My Call

What is your dream?

What do you really dream about being and doing—at those times when you are all alone and have plenty of time to think? If you know the answer to that you know a great deal about yourself. And about the way you look at the world.

Most people have a dream. They have somewhere in the back of their minds a dream of someday accomplishing something great. Perhaps they even dream of influencing the world.

Some people realize their dreams. They do accomplish great things—or at least those things which they have defined as being great—and some do influence the world, for good or bad.

But there are other people who feel trapped by life. They have lost their ability to dream. They feel closed in. They have lost the hope that they could effectively influence the world.

Whichever of these groups you are in, God is ready to meet you—whenever you turn in His direction. If you already have dreams He may change them, or give you larger ones. Or if you have lost hope of doing anything significant in this world, He can show you what you can do.

The fact is, God deals with ordinary people. When Jesus was on earth in the flesh, He loved to talk with, and work with, ordinary people. Read Mark 1:16–22. He made it a point to spend time with them. And in doing this He often bypassed those who were overly impressed with their own importance.

And when Jesus chose men to be with Him, to train under Him, to prepare to influence the world, He chose very ordinary men. Fishermen. A tax collector. And so it went. Ordinary people. He showed them the path to real significance. And that was the path to fellowship with His Father.

Jesus still chooses ordinary men. In fact, even great men, by the world's estimation, must become ordinary men in order to find Him.

Once you find Him, you hear Him saying "Follow me," and it requires a decision. If you go on doing what you have always done, being what you have always been, seeing things as you have always seen them, it is certain that you have never really met Him. Once you follow Him, everything changes. And you know it.

In finding Him you find your calling.

Know the Work

The trouble with much training, much of what passes for education, is that it leads nowhere.

Abstract, unrelated knowledge can have its values. There is a great place for "basic research." But there must eventually be some point at which education relates to action. Otherwise the value of knowledge may be questioned.

From reading the Gospels it appears that much of the time of the disciples was taken up in watching Jesus, absorbing His attitudes, getting to know His approach to situations, seeing Him react to problems. And this must have had tremendous value in their subsequent ministry. Read Mark 6:7–13.

At times, in later years, it actually appeared that the disciples had absorbed enough of Jesus' attitudes, enough of His approach to problems, that people were impressed that they had in fact been with Jesus and were trained by Him. (See Acts 4:13.)

Yet even while they were with Jesus, the disciples were given opportunity to put into practice the things they had learned from their Master. One occasion is the focus of our reading for today.

In sending out the twelve to the villages around, Jesus did two things. He gave them special powers, and He took away all superfluous dependencies. Both were aimed at trusting Him to supply the needs, both material and spiritual. It was one way of bringing them to test their reliance upon Him, and perhaps also to test the training He had given them to that point. God would use them, just as He used Jesus, as long as their outlook, their dependence, their sense of the source of power was the same as Jesus' had been.

It is always tempting to trust things other than God, and quite apart from God. We tend to expect results in line with the normal pattern of cause and effect. We put this in, and we get that out. Right?

Wrong! At least, if we leave God out of the formula, we are bound to be wrong. What He seems to want most is our genuine dependence on Him. That comes far ahead of our brilliance, or our capabilities of various sorts. He really wants our attitude of reliance on Him ahead of everything else.

So we find, as the disciples did, that to know the work is to know Jesus and His attitude toward what must be done in declaring God's truth to men.

Know the People

One thing is unmistakable about Jesus' life on earth. He knew people, and He knew them well. He had penetrating insights into the thoughts and inner feelings of those with whom He came in contact. And it was often that element of His approach that drew people to Him personally.

Take the woman at the well, for instance. (See John 4.) He knew her thoughts, her motivations, and even her history. This was so true that the woman said later to others, "Come, see a man, which told me all things that ever I did" (John 4:29).

The followers of Jesus might be expected to share something of this ability to see into men—or at least to be sensitive to what they say and feel. That is a good point of beginning. Jesus was constantly attuned to people. He listened to what they said, and felt what they seemed to feel. Yet all too often we shut other people out. We live so much within ourselves that we have difficulties really hearing other people. We are so often bad listeners.

There is a suggestion in Mark's Gospel (6:30–34) that the disciples had some degree of success in their mission, as they reported it to Jesus. They had found people in need, and they had been effective in solving some of the problems they encountered. They had preached repentance, healed some that were sick, and now they were exhausted. And Jesus suggested that they go apart to rest. He knew His followers well enough to see they needed it.

But the crowds managed to find them, and

would not let them alone. And so Jesus looked out on the crowds and He pitied them. It was as though He could see right through them—their needs, their desires, their helplessness, their lostness, their frustrations, their guilt, their loneliness. He saw them as sheep being scattered, having no one to care for them, nobody to lead them, nobody to guide them to the light.

Again Jesus was involved in meeting the needs, until He had no rest whatever, not enough time even to eat. Here, out in the desert, people were pressing in upon Him, eager to get His help, His blessing, His healing, His teaching. But it was too much for the disciples, who were weary and hungry.

Yet again we find Jesus attuned to the real need, the problem of that moment. The people were hungry, and Jesus knew it. And He still had the resources to meet that need—which led Him to feed the fiive thousand.

Know My Goal

Christians tend to be isolationists. We think in individualistic terms, about ourselves and our own individual lives, rather than about the group or the society or the total environment to which we belong. This is a tendency, not a generalization that holds in every case.

Our tendency toward individualism has carried over into our understanding of the church, and how the church should be, and how it should act within the world, or at least our part of the world.

Thus when we think of the church, we think of ourselves, plus a lot of other people who are individuals like ourselves. We assume that they must have the same kinds of feelings and reactions to things, and the same outlook on what is going on. And then we take a look at reality and we find out that it is not that way at all. And we tend to be disappointed because there is as much variety of opinion and even of action within the church as there is outside it.

We have not thought enough about mutual relationships, or of mutual concerns, or of mutual growth, or of mutual training in the way that we ought to. Consequently we are living with problems in the church which result from our subconscious attitudes which we carry into the church from our cultural situation.

Cultural influence in the church is nothing new, and it is certainly not limited to our Western culture. The point here is that we tend to have an individualistic outlook.

Paul gives us a viewpoint in Ephesians 4:11—16 which will help correct our individualism. He is stressing that the body of Christ, the church, is much like the human body. It has many members, and many of them are very different from each other and have different functions. But the differences are good. They make for the total upbuilding of the church in the long run.

In this case Paul is talking about different gifts and capabilities which relate to specific offices and roles in the church. But he is not leaving anyone out, for he goes on to stress that these servants or ministers are given their role so that others might be built up and trained for a ministry of their own.

The object of it all is maturity. That is the answer to weakness in the church, and it is the best way to insure against falling into error.

Know the Requirements

Christianity was never meant to be a spectator sport, but it has often become that. Christian faith is something a lot of people slip into on a Sunday morning, as they enter the sanctuary for worship. But they slip it off again, just as easily. And that does it. It is a marginal activity in their lives.

Paul describes the Christian life as a race—definitely a participation sport, and a full-time pursuit. See II Timothy 2:1–7. It requires us to "be strong" in the faith that is in Jesus Christ. This is where the training program comes in. It is necessary to build up that strength in the faith.

Yet, how much of this sort of training do most Christians get today? In most church activities, do you find that things are set toward producing really strong Christians—men and women who are able to lead others to the strength of the faith in Christ?

How can our training programs get set (or reset) to accomplish that?

The remedy must be related to taking seriously the fact of being a Christian. Our cultural situation does not encourage this. It is the easier thing, the more expected thing, that people will take their religion (whatever their preference may be) in small doses. Just enough to make them feel reasonably good about things in general. But don't become a fanatic!

Yet the biblical picture seems to say the opposite. Give your whole life and existence to what you are in Christ. That suggests a fanatic. And Christ needs people today who are willing to be fanatic about their faith in Him—but expressing it in a way that is fully in keeping with the fact that He is God.

Any training program that will be worth anything at all, must be geared to that outlook. So, if you are involved in the Christian race, train and run to win. You must mean business about it. And if you are enlisted as "a good soldier of Christ Jesus" you need to go right through basic training, specialized training, and then into the battle. Be prepared to serve with all that you are, and be willing to get involved in training others to serve Him with a similar seriousness.

If we get that kind of a training program going, things will be sure to happen!

Keep the Perspective

Sound judgment—good sense—wisdom—really understanding the situation—knowing what the problem is—ability to see where any action will lead—acquiring the knowledge on which to make a proper decision—courage to take the right course: these are the qualities that count in the long run.

Any businessman, or military officer, or statesman could look over that list and agree with it fully. In one sense, the quality of good judgment applies as much in the world as it does in the church.

Yet there is a difference. And that difference involves the Christian perspective on the real nature of the world. To the Christian the things that count most in the long run are the things that are "not seen."

Paul puts this clearly, after reciting all the problems and physical harassments which he had encountered. "While we look not at the things which are seen, but at the things which are not seen: for the things which are seen are temporal; but the things which are not seen are eternal" (II Corinthians 4:18).

That is the Christian perspective. And wisdom as the Christian knows and expresses it must be based on that perspective. It is a dimension that relates to the Christian, but the world—without Christ—cannot understand that viewpoint. It is a dimension of things that is simply not available to the person outside Christ. Yet it is upon that perspective that real wisdom is based.

Training is necessary to develop and maintain that outlook. It comes from first taking Jesus Christ seriously, and then from soaking ourselves in the Word that He has given us. And it can be encouraged and strengthened through contacts with others who have managed to see the world of the "unseen but real."

You should be on both ends of the training process—receiving it, and giving it. Are you? What, exactly, has been your training in the Christian life? Are you in continual education as far as your Christian life is concerned? Should you be taking a brush-up course?

And what training are you providing for others? Who looks to you as his coach? Is the course that you have laid out for him designed so that he can measure growth and development—so as to get the before-and-after picture?

Perhaps the most important need of all in the church today is the need to develop followers of Jesus who have this perspective, and live by it. That is what it means to run the Christian race, to fight the Christian warfare, to do the work of Christ in this world. For all the other elements of the Christian life take their shape around this perspective—the perspective of faith.